RESUMES
FOR
NURSING
CAREERS

VGM Professional Resumes Series

RESUMES FOR NURSING CAREERS

The Editors of
VGM Career Books

Second Edition, With Sample Cover Letters

VGM Career Books

Chicago   New York   San Francisco   Lisbon   London   Madrid   Mexico City
Milan   New Delhi   San Juan   Seoul   Singapore   Sydney   Toronto

Library of Congress Cataloging-in-Publication Data

Resumes for nursing careers / the editors of VGM Career Books. — 2nd ed.
      p.   cm. — (VGM professional resumes series)
    ISBN 0-658-01772-1
     1. Nurses—Employment.   2. Résumés (Employment)   3. Nursing—Vocational
series.   I. Title.   II. Series.

RT86.7 .R45   2001
610.73′06′9—dc21   2001026431

VGM Career Books

A Division of The McGraw·Hill Companies

*The editors gratefully acknowledge the assistance of Megan Phillips
in the compiling and editing of this book.*

ISBN 0-658-01772-1

This book was set in Minion by Ellen Kollmon
Printed and bound by Vicks Lithograph

McGraw-Hill books are available at special quantity discounts to use as premiums and
sales promotions, or for use in corporate training programs. For more information, please
write to the Director of Special Sales, Professional Publishing, McGraw-Hill, Two Penn
Plaza, New York, NY 10121-2298. Or contact your local bookstore.

This book is printed on acid-free paper.

Contents

Introduction

Your resume is a piece of paper (or an electronic document) that serves to introduce you to the people who will eventually hire you. To write a thoughtful resume, you must thoroughly assess your personality, your accomplishments, and the skills you have acquired. The act of composing and submitting a resume also requires you to carefully consider the company or individual that might hire you. What are they looking for, and how can you meet their needs? This book shows you how to organize your personal information and experience into a concise and well-written resume, so that your qualifications and potential as an employee will be understood easily and quickly by a complete stranger.

Writing the resume is just one step in what can be a daunting job-search process, but it is an important element in the chain of events that will lead you to your new position. While you are probably a talented, bright, and charming person, your resume may not reflect these qualities. A poorly written resume can get you nowhere; a well-written resume can land you an interview and potentially a job. A good resume can even lead the interviewer to ask you questions that will allow you to talk about your strengths and highlight the skills you can bring to a prospective employer. Even a person with very little experience can find a good job if he or she is assisted by a thoughtful and polished resume.

Lengthy, typewritten resumes are a thing of the past. Today, employers do not have the time or the patience for verbose documents; they look for tightly composed, straightforward, action-based resumes. Although a one-page resume is the norm, a two-page resume may be warranted if you have had extensive job experience or have changed careers and truly need the space to properly position yourself. If, after careful editing, you still need more than one page to present yourself, it's acceptable to use a second page. A crowded resume that's hard to read would be the worst of your choices.

Distilling your work experience, education, and interests into such a small space requires preparation and thought. This book takes you step-by-step through the process of crafting an effective resume that will stand out in today's competitive marketplace. It serves as a workbook and a place to write down your experiences, while also including the techniques you'll need to pull all the necessary elements together. In the following pages, you'll find many examples of resumes that are specific to your area of interest. Study them for inspiration and find what appeals to you. There are a variety of ways to organize and present your information; inside, you'll find several that will be suitable to your needs. Good luck landing the job of your dreams!

RESUMES
FOR
NURSING
CAREERS

The Elements of an Effective Resume

An effective resume is composed of information that employers are most interested in knowing about a prospective job applicant. This information is conveyed by a few essential elements. The following is a list of elements that are found in most resumes—some essential, some optional. Later in this chapter, we will further examine the role of each of these elements in the makeup of your resume.

- Heading

- Objective and/or Keyword Section

- Work Experience

- Education

- Honors

- Activities

- Certificates and Licenses

- Publications

- Professional Memberships

- Special Skills

- Personal Information

- References

The first step in preparing your resume is to gather information about yourself and your past accomplishments. Later you will refine this information, rewrite it using effective language, and organize it into an attractive layout. But first, let's take a look at each of these important elements individually so you can judge their appropriateness for your resume.

Heading

Although the heading may be seem to be the simplest section of your resume, be careful not to take it lightly. It is the first section your prospective employer will see and it contains the information she or he will need to contact you. At the very least, the heading must contain your name, your home address, and, of course, a phone number where you can be reached easily.

In today's high-tech world, many of us have multiple ways that we can be contacted. You may list your E-mail address if you are reasonably sure the employer makes use of this form of communication. Keep in mind, however, that others may have access to your E-mail messages if you send them from an account provided by your current company. If this is a concern, do not list your work E-mail address on your resume. If you are able to take calls at your current place of business, you should include your work number, because most employers will attempt to contact you during typical business hours.

If you have voice mail or a reliable answering machine at home or at work, list its number in the heading and make sure your greeting is professional and clear. Always include at least one phone number in your heading, even if it is a temporary number, where a prospective employer can leave a message.

You might have a dozen different ways to be contacted, but you do not need to list all of them. Confine your numbers or addresses to those that are the easiest for the prospective employer to use and the simplest for you to retrieve.

Objective

When seeking a specific career path, it is important to list a job or career objective on your resume. This statement helps employers know the direction you see yourself taking, so they can determine whether your goals are in line with those of their organization and the position available. Normally, an objective is one to two sentences long. Its contents will vary depending on your career field, goals, and personality. The objective can be specific or general, but it should always be to the point. See the sample resumes in this book for examples.

If you are planning to use this resume on-line, or you suspect your potential employer is likely to scan your resume, you will want to include a "keyword" in the objective. This allows a prospective employer, searching hundreds of resumes for a specific skill or position objective, to locate the keyword and find your resume. In essence, a keyword is what's "hot" in your particular field at a given time. It's a buzzword, a shorthand way of getting a particular message across at a glance. For example, if you are a lawyer, your objective might state your desire to work in the area of corporate litigation. In this case, someone searching for the keyword "corporate litigation" will pull up your resume and know that you want to plan, research, and present cases at trial on behalf of the corporation. If your objective states that you "desire a challenging position in systems design," the keyword is "systems design," an industry-specific, shorthand way of saying that you want to be involved in assessing the need for, acquiring, and implementing high-technology systems. These are keywords and every industry has them, so it's becoming more and more important to include a few in your resume. (You may need to conduct additional research to make sure you know what keywords are most likely to be used in your desired industry, profession, or situation.)

There are many resume and job-search sites on-line. Like most things in the on-line world, they vary a great deal in quality. Use your discretion. If you plan to apply for jobs on-line or advertise your availability this way, you will want to design a scannable resume. This type of resume uses a format that can be easily scanned into a computer and added to a database. Scanning allows a prospective employer to use keywords to quickly review each applicant's experience and skills, and (in the event that there are many candidates for the job) to keep your resume for future reference.

Many people find that it is worthwhile to create two or more versions of their basic resume. You may want an intricately designed resume on high-quality paper to mail or hand out *and* a resume that is designed to be scanned into a computer and saved on a database or an on-line job site. You can even create a resume in ASCII text to E-mail to prospective employers. For further information, you may wish to refer to *The Guide to Internet Job Searching*, by Frances Roehm and Margaret Dikel, updated and published every other year by VGM Career Books, a division of the McGraw-Hill Companies. This excellent book contains helpful and detailed information about formatting a resume for Internet use. To get you started, in Chapter 3 we have included a list of things to keep in mind when creating electronic resumes.

Although it is usually a good idea to include an objective, in some cases this element is not necessary. The goal of the objective statement is to provide the employer with an idea of where you see yourself going in the field. However, if you are uncertain of the exact nature of the job you seek, including an objective that is too specific could result in your not being considered for a host of perfectly acceptable positions. If you decide not to use an objective heading in your resume, you should definitely incorporate the information that would be conveyed in the objective into your cover letter.

Work Experience

Work experience is arguably the most important element of them all. Unless you are a recent graduate with little or no relevant work experience, your current and former positions will provide the central focus of the resume. You will want this section to be as complete and carefully constructed as possible. By thoroughly examining your work experience, you can get to the heart of your accomplishments and present them in a way that demonstrates and highlights your qualifications.

If you are just out of school, your resume will probably focus on your education, but you should also include information on your work or volunteer experiences. Although you will have less information about work experience than a person who has held multiple positions or is advanced in his or her career, the amount of information is not what is most important in this section. How the information is presented and what it says about you as a worker and a person is what really counts.

As you create this section of your resume, remember the need for accuracy. Include all the necessary information about each of your jobs, including your job title, dates of employment, name of your employer, city, state, responsibilities, special projects you handled, and accomplishments. Be sure to list only accomplishments for which you were directly responsible. And don't be alarmed if you haven't participated in or worked on special projects, because this section may not be relevant to certain jobs.

The most common way to list your work experience is in *reverse chronological order*. In other words, start with your most recent job and work your way backward. This way, your prospective employer sees your current (and often most important) position before considering your past employment. Your most recent position, if it's the most important in terms of responsibilities and relevance to the job for which you are applying, should also be the one that includes the most information as compared to your previous positions.

If you are just out of school, highlight your summer employment, internships, and part-time work. As a recent graduate, however, you will probably begin your resume with your education section. The experience you gain with "starter jobs" in the workplace and your ability to juggle school and employment are important to most employers, even if the work itself seems unrelated to your proposed career path. If you were promoted or given greater responsibilities or commendations, be sure to mention this important fact.

The following worksheet is provided to help you organize your experiences in the working world. It will also serve as an excellent resource to refer to when updating your resume in the future.

WORK EXPERIENCE

Job One:

Job Title _____

Dates _____

Employer _____

City, State _____

Major Duties _____

_____

_____

_____

_____

_____

_____

_____

_____

Special Projects _____

_____

_____

_____

Accomplishments _____

_____

_____

_____

_____

_____

_____

_____

Job Two:

Job Title _____

Dates _____

Employer _____

City, State _____

Major Duties _____

_____

_____

_____

_____

_____

_____

_____

_____

Special Projects _____

_____

_____

_____

Accomplishments _____

_____

_____

_____

_____

_____

_____

_____

_____

_____

Job Three:

Job Title _____

Dates _____

Employer _____

City, State _____

Major Duties _____

_____

_____

_____

_____

_____

_____

_____

Special Projects _____

_____

_____

_____

Accomplishments _____

_____

_____

_____

_____

_____

_____

_____

_____

Job Four:

Job Title _____

Dates _____

Employer _____

City, State _____

Major Duties _____

_____

_____

_____

_____

_____

_____

_____

_____

Special Projects _____

_____

_____

_____

Accomplishments _____

_____

_____

_____

_____

_____

_____

_____

Education

Education is usually the second most important element of a resume. Your educational background is often a deciding factor in an employer's decision to interview you. Highlight your accomplishments in school as much as you did those at work. If you are looking for your first professional job, your education will be your greatest asset, because your related work experience will probably be minimal. In this case, the education section becomes the most important means of selling yourself.

Include in this section all the degrees or certificates you have received; your major or area of concentration; all of the honors you earned; and any relevant activities you participated in, organized, or chaired. Again, list your most recent schooling first. If you have completed graduate-level work, begin with that and work your way back through your undergraduate education. If you have completed college, you generally should not list your high school experience; do so only if you earned special honors, you had a grade point average that was much better than the norm, or this was your highest level of education.

If you have completed a large number of credit hours in a subject that may be relevant to the position you are seeking, but did not obtain a degree, you may wish to list the hours or classes you completed. Keep in mind, however, that you may be asked to explain why you did not finish the program. If you are currently in school, list the degree, certificate, or license you expect to obtain and the projected date of completion.

The following worksheet will help you gather the information you need for this section of your resume.

EDUCATION

School One _____

Major or Area of Concentration _____

Degree _____

Dates _____

School Two _____

Major or Area of Concentration _____

Degree _____

Dates _____

Honors

If you include an honors section in your resume, you should highlight any awards, honors, or memberships in honorary societies that you have received. (You may also incorporate this information into your education section.) Often, the honors are academic in nature, but this section also may be used for special achievements in sports, clubs, or other school activities. Always include the name of the organization awarding the honor and the date(s) received. Use the following worksheet to help you gather your information.

HONORS

Honor One _____

Awarding Organization _____

Date(s) _____

Honor Two _____

Awarding Organization _____

Date(s) _____

Honor Three _____

Awarding Organization _____

Date(s) _____

Honor Four _____

Awarding Organization _____

Date(s) _____

Honor Five _____

Awarding Organization _____

Date(s) _____

Activities

Perhaps you were active in different organizations or clubs during your years at school; often an employer will look at such involvement as evidence of initiative, dedication, and good social skills. Examples of your ability to take a leading role in a group should be included on a resume, if you can provide them. (Information about your activities also may be incorporated into your education section.) If you have been out of school for some time, the activities section of your resume can present neighborhood and community activities, volunteer positions, and so forth. In general, you may want to avoid listing any organization whose name indicates the race, creed, sex, age, marital status, sexual orientation, or nation of origin of its members, because this could expose you to discrimination. Use the following worksheet to list the specifics of your activities.

ACTIVITIES

Organization/Activity _____

Accomplishments _____

_____

_____

Organization/Activity _____

Accomplishments _____

_____

_____

Organization/Activity _____

Accomplishments _____

_____

_____

As your work experience grows through the years, your school activities and honors will carry less weight and be emphasized less in your resume. Eventually, you will probably list only your degree and any major honors received. As time goes by, your job performance and the experience you've gained become the most important elements in your resume, which should change to reflect this.

Certificates and Licenses

If your chosen career path requires specialized training, you may already have certificates or licenses. You should list these if the job you are seeking requires them and you, of course, have acquired them. If you have applied for a license but have not yet received it, use the phrase "application pending."

License requirements vary by state. If you have moved or are planning to relocate to another state, check with that state's board or licensing agency for all licensing requirements.

Always make sure that all of the information you list is completely accurate. Locate copies of your certificates and licenses, and check the exact date and name of the accrediting agency. Use the following worksheet to organize the necessary information.

CERTIFICATES AND LICENSES

Name of License _____

Licensing Agency _____

Date Issued _____

Name of License _____

Licensing Agency _____

Date Issued _____

Name of License _____

Licensing Agency _____

Date Issued _____

Publications

Some professions strongly encourage or even require that you publish. If you have written, coauthored, or edited any books, articles, professional papers, or works of a similar nature that pertain to your field, you will definitely want to include this element. Remember to list the date of publication and the publisher's name, and specify whether you were the sole author or a coauthor. Book, magazine, or journal titles are generally italicized, while the titles of articles within a larger publication appear in quotes. (Check with your reference librarian for more about the appropriate way to present this information.) For scientific or research papers, you will need to give the date, place, and audience to whom the paper was presented.

Use the following worksheet to help you gather the necessary information about your publications.

PUBLICATIONS

Title and Type (Note, Article, Etc.) _____

Title of Publication (Journal, Book, Etc.) _____

Publisher _____

Date Published _____

Title and Type (Note, Article, Etc.) _____

Title of Publication (Journal, Book, Etc.) _____

Publisher _____

Date Published _____

Title and Type (Note, Article, Etc.) _____

Title of Publication (Journal, Book, Etc.) _____

Publisher _____

Date Published _____

Professional Memberships

Another potential element in your resume is a section listing professional memberships. Use this section to describe your involvement in professional associations, unions, and similar organizations. It is to your advantage to list any professional memberships that pertain to the job you are seeking. Many employers see your membership as representative of your desire to stay up-to-date and connected in your field. Include the dates of your involvement and whether you took part in any special activities or held any offices within the organization. Use the following worksheet to organize your information.

PROFESSIONAL MEMBERSHIPS

Name of Organization _____

Office(s) Held_____

Activities _____

Dates _____

Name of Organization _____

Office(s) Held_____

Activities _____

Dates _____

Name of Organization _____

Office(s) Held_____

Activities _____

Dates _____

Name of Organization _____

Office(s) Held_____

Activities _____

Dates _____

Special Skills

The special skills section of your resume is the place to mention any special abilities you have that relate to the job you are seeking. You can use this element to present certain talents or experiences that are not necessarily a part of your education or work experience. Common examples include fluency in a foreign language, extensive travel abroad, or knowledge of a particular computer application. "Special skills" can encompass a wide range of talents, and this section can be used creatively. However, for each skill you list, you should be able to describe how it would be a direct asset in the type of work you're seeking, because employers may ask just that in an interview. If you can't think of a way to do this, it may be extraneous information.

Personal Information

Some people include personal information on their resumes. This is generally not recommended, but you might wish to include it if you think that something in your personal life, such as a hobby or talent, has some bearing on the position you are seeking. This type of information is often referred to at the beginning of an interview, when it may be used as an "icebreaker." Of course, personal information regarding your age, marital status, race, religion, or sexual orientation should never appear on your resume as *personal information*. It should be given only in the context of memberships and activities, and only when doing so would not expose you to discrimination.

References

References are not usually given on the resume itself, but a prospective employer needs to know that you have references who may be contacted if necessary. All you need to include is a single sentence at the end of the resume: "References are available upon request," or even simply, "References available." Have a reference list ready—your interviewer may ask to see it! Contact each person on the list ahead of time to see whether it is all right for you to use him or her as a reference. This way, the person has a chance to think about what to say *before* the call occurs. This helps ensure that you will obtain the best reference possible.

Chapter 2

Writing Your Resume

Now that you have gathered the information for each section of your resume, it's time to write it out in a way that will get the attention of the reviewer—hopefully, your future employer! The language you use in your resume will affect its success, so you must be careful and conscientious. Translate the facts you have gathered into the active, precise language of resume writing. You will be aiming for a resume that keeps the reader's interest and highlights your accomplishments in a concise and effective way.

Resume writing is unlike any other form of writing. Although your seventh-grade composition teacher would not approve, the rules of punctuation and sentence building are often completely ignored. Instead, you should try for a functional, direct writing style that focuses on the use of verbs and other words that imply action on your part. Writing with action words and strong verbs characterizes you to potential employers as an energetic, active person, someone who completes tasks and achieves results from his or her work. Resumes that do not make use of action words can sound passive and stale. These resumes are not effective and do not get the attention of any employer, no matter how qualified the applicant. Choose words that display your strengths and demonstrate your initiative. The following list of commonly used verbs will help you create a strong resume:

administered	assembled
advised	assumed responsibility
analyzed	billed
arranged	built

carried out	inspected
channeled	interviewed
collected	introduced
communicated	invented
compiled	maintained
completed	managed
conducted	met with
contacted	motivated
contracted	negotiated
coordinated	operated
counseled	orchestrated
created	ordered
cut	organized
designed	oversaw
determined	performed
developed	planned
directed	prepared
dispatched	presented
distributed	produced
documented	programmed
edited	published
established	purchased
expanded	recommended
functioned as	recorded
gathered	reduced
handled	referred
hired	represented
implemented	researched
improved	reviewed

saved	supervised
screened	taught
served as	tested
served on	trained
sold	typed
suggested	wrote

Let's look at two examples that differ only in their writing style. The first resume section is ineffective because it does not use action words to accent the applicant's work experiences:

WORK EXPERIENCE
Regional Sales Manager

Manager of sales representatives from seven states. Manager of twelve food chain accounts in the East. In charge of the sales force's planned selling toward specific goals. Supervisor and trainer of new sales representatives. Consulting for customers in the areas of inventory management and quality control.

Special Projects: Coordinator and sponsor of annual food industry sales seminar.

Accomplishments: Monthly regional volume went up 25 percent during my tenure while, at the same time, a proper sales/cost ratio was maintained. Customer-company relations were improved.

In the following paragraph, we have rewritten the same section using action words. Notice how the tone has changed. It now sounds stronger and more active. This person accomplished goals and really *did* things.

WORK EXPERIENCE
Regional Sales Manager

Managed sales representatives from seven states. Oversaw twelve food chain accounts in the eastern United States. Directed the sales force in planned selling toward specific goals. Supervised and trained new sales representatives. Counseled customers in the areas of inventory management and quality control. Coordinated and sponsored the annual Food Industry Seminar. Increased monthly regional volume 25 percent and helped to improve customer-company relations during my tenure.

One helpful way to construct the work experience section is to make use of your actual job descriptions—the written duties and expectations your employers had for a person in your current or former position. Job descriptions are rarely written in proper resume language, so you will have to rework them, but they do include much of the information necessary to create this section of your resume. If you have access to job descriptions for your former positions, you can use the details to construct an action-oriented paragraph. Often, your human resources department can provide a job description for your current position.

The following is an example of a typical human resources job description, followed by a rewritten version of the same description employing action words and specific details about the job. Again, pay attention to the style of writing instead of the content, as the details of your own experience will be unique.

WORK EXPERIENCE
Public Administrator I

Responsibilities: Coordinate and direct public services to meet the needs of the nation, state, or community. Analyze problems; work with special committees and public agencies; recommend solutions to governing bodies.

Aptitudes and Skills: Ability to relate to and communicate with people; solve complex problems through analysis; plan, organize, and implement policies and programs. Knowledge of political systems, financial management, personnel administration, program evaluation, and organizational theory.

WORK EXPERIENCE
Public Administrator I

Wrote pamphlets and conducted discussion groups to inform citizens of legislative processes and consumer issues. Organized and supervised 25 interviewers. Trained interviewers in effective communication skills.

After you have written out your resume, you are ready to begin the next important step: assembly and layout.

Chapter 3

Assembly and Layout

At this point, you've gathered all the necessary information for your resume and rewritten it in language that will impress your potential employers. Your next step is to assemble the sections in a logical order and lay them out on the page neatly and attractively to achieve the desired effect: getting the interview.

Assembly

The order of the elements in a resume makes a difference in its overall effect. Clearly, you would not want to bury your name and address somewhere in the middle of the resume. Nor would you want to lead with a less important section, such as special skills. Put the elements in an order that stresses your most important accomplishments and the things that will be most appealing to your potential employer. For example, if you recently graduated from school and have no full-time work experience, you will want the reviewer to read about your education before any part-time jobs you may have held during the vacations. On the other hand, if you have been gainfully employed for several years and currently hold an important position in your company, you should list your work accomplishments ahead of your educational information, which has become less pertinent with time.

Certain things should always be included in your resume, but others are optional. The following list shows you which are which. You might want to use it as a checklist to be certain that you have included all of the necessary information.

Essential	Optional
Name	Cellular Phone Number
Address	Pager Number
Phone Number	E-mail Address or Website Address
Work Experience	Voice Mail Number
Education	Job Objective
References Phrase	Honors
	Special Skills
	Publications
	Professional Memberships
	Activities
	Certificates and Licenses
	Personal Information
	Graphics
	Photograph

Your choice of optional sections depends on your own background and employment needs. Always use information that will put you in a favorable light—unless it's absolutely essential, avoid anything that will prompt the interviewer to ask questions about your weaknesses or something else that could be unflattering. Make sure your information is accurate and truthful. If your honors are impressive, include them in the resume. If your activities in school demonstrate talents that are necessary for the job you are seeking, allow space for a section on activities. If you are applying for a position that requires ornamental illustration, you may want to include border illustrations or graphics that demonstrate your talents in this area. If you are answering an advertisement for a job that requires certain physical traits, a photo of yourself might be appropriate. A person applying for a job as a computer programmer would *not* include a photo as part of his or her resume. Each resume is unique, just as each person is unique.

Types of Resumes

So far we have focused on the most common type of resume—the *reverse chronological* resume—in which your most recent job is listed first. This is the type of resume usually preferred by those who have to read a large number of resumes, and it is by far the most popular and widely circulated. However, this style of presentation may not be the most effective way to highlight *your* skills and accomplishments.

For example, if you are reentering the workforce after many years or are trying to change career fields, the *functional* resume may work best. This type of resume puts the focus on your achievements instead of the sequence of your work history. In the functional resume, your experience is presented through your general accomplishments and the skills you have developed in your working life.

A functional resume is assembled from the same information you gathered in Chapter 1. The main difference lies in how you organize the information. Essentially, the work experience section is divided in two, with your job duties and accomplishments constituting one section and your employers' names, cities, and states; your positions; and the dates employed making up the other. Place the first section near the top of your resume, just below your job objective (if used), and call it *Accomplishments* or *Achievements*. The second section, containing the bare essentials of your work history, should come after the accomplishments section and can be called *Employment History*, since it is a chronological overview of your former jobs.

The other sections of your resume remain the same. The work experience section is the only one affected in the functional format. By placing the section that focuses on your achievements at the beginning, you draw attention to these achievements. This puts less emphasis on whom you worked for and when, and more on what you did and what you are capable of doing.

If you are changing careers, the emphasis on skills and achievements is important. The identities of previous employers (who aren't part of your new career field) need to be downplayed. A functional resume can help accomplish this task. If you are reentering the workforce after a long absence, a functional resume is the obvious choice. And if you lack full-time work experience, you will need to draw attention away from this fact and put the focus on your skills and abilities. You may need to highlight your volunteer activities and part-time work. Education may also play a more important role in your resume.

The type of resume that is right for you will depend on your personal circumstances. It may be helpful to create both types and then compare them. Which one presents you in the best light? Examples of both types of resumes are included in this book. Use the sample resumes in Chapter 5 to help you decide on the content, presentation, and look of your own resume.

Special Tips for Electronic Resumes

Because there are many details to consider in writing a resume that will be posted or transmitted on the Internet, or one that will be scanned into a computer when it is received, we suggest that you refer to *The Guide to Internet Job Searching*, by Frances Roehm and Margaret Dikel, as previously mentioned. However, here are some brief, general guidelines to follow if you expect your resume to be scanned into a computer.

- Use standard fonts in which none of the letters touch.

- Keep in mind that underlining, italics, and fancy scripts may not scan well.

- Use boldface and capitalization to set off elements. Again, make sure letters don't touch. Leave at least a quarter inch between lines of type.

- Keep information and elements at the left margin. Centering, columns, and even indenting may change when the resume is optically scanned.

- Do not use any lines, boxes, or graphics.

- Place the most important information at the top of the first page. If you use two pages, put your name and "Page 2 of 2" at the top of the second page.

- List each telephone number on its own line in the header.

- Use multiple keywords or synonyms for what you do to make sure your qualifications will be picked up if a prospective employer is searching for them. Use nouns that are keywords for your profession.

- Be descriptive in your titles. For example, don't just use "assistant"; use "legal office assistant."

- Make sure the contrast between print and paper is good. Use a high-quality laser printer and white or very light-colored 8½-by-11-inch paper.

- Mail a high-quality laser print or an excellent copy. Do not fold or use staples, as this might interfere with scanning. You may, however, use paper clips.

In addition to creating a resume that works well for scanning, you may want to have a resume that can be E-mailed to reviewers. Because you may not know what word processing application the recipient uses, the best format to use is ASCII text. (ASCII stands for "American Standard Code for Information Exchange.") It allows people with very different software platforms to exchange and understand information. (E-mail operates on this principle.) ASCII is a simple, text-only language, which means you can include only simple text. There can be no use of boldface, italics, or even paragraph indentations.

To create an ASCII resume, just use your normal word processing program; when finished, save it as a "text only" document. You will find this option under the "save" or "save as" command. Here is a list of things to *avoid* when crafting your electronic resume:

- Tabs. Use your space bar. Tabs will not work.

- Any special characters, such as mathematical symbols.

- Word wrap. Use hard returns (the return key) to make line breaks.

- Centering or other formatting. Align everything at the left margin.

- Bold or italic fonts. Everything will be converted to plain text when you save the file as a "text only" document.

Check carefully for any mistakes before you save the document as a text file. Spellcheck and proofread it several times, then ask someone with a keen eye to go over it for you again. Remember: the key is to keep it simple. Any attempt to make this resume pretty or decorative may result in a resume that is confusing and hard to read. After you have saved the document, you can cut and paste it into an E-mail or onto a website.

Layout for a Paper Resume

A great deal of care—and much more formatting—is necessary to achieve an attractive layout for your paper resume. There is no single appropriate layout that applies to every resume, but there are a few basic rules to follow in putting your resume on paper:

- Leave a comfortable margin on the sides, top, and bottom of the page (usually one to one and a half inches).

- Use appropriate spacing between the sections (two to three line spaces are usually adequate).

- Be consistent in the *type* of headings you use for different sections of your resume. For example, if you capitalize the heading EMPLOYMENT HISTORY, don't use initial capitals and underlining for a section of equal importance, such as <u>Education</u>.

- Do not use more than one font in your resume. Stay consistent by choosing a font that is fairly standard and easy to read, and don't change it for different sections. Beware of the tendency to try to make your resume original by choosing fancy type styles; your resume may end up looking unprofessional instead of creative. Unless you are in a very creative and artistic field, you should almost always stick with tried-and-true type styles like Times New Roman and Palatino, which are often used in business writing. In the area of resume styles, conservative is usually the best way to go.

- Always try to fit your resume on one page. If you are having trouble with this, you may be trying to say too much. Edit out any repetitive or unnecessary information, and shorten descriptions of earlier jobs where possible. Ask a friend you trust for feedback on what seems unnecessary or unimportant. For example, you may have included too many optional sections. Today, with the prevalence of the personal computer as a tool, there is no excuse for a poorly laid-out resume. Experiment with variations until you are pleased with the result.

CHRONOLOGICAL RESUME

INDIRA PAX   988 Gavin Road
Newport News, VA 23606
Home (904) 555-8214
Cellular (904) 555-9602

Goal: Management position in home health industry that will use supervisory and marketing skills.

Experience:

9/98 to Present   **Director of Recruitment, NurseTemps Inc.**
Direct marketing/recruitment program. Design direct mail campaigns. Produce promotional literature. Developed employee screening process currently in use. Monitor employee performance. Have increased staffing by 15 percent during past year.

8/95 to 9/98   **Educational Director, St. Anne's Hospital**
Responsible for staff orientation, peer review, and community outreach programs.

7/91 to 8/95   **Director of Nursing, Morgan County Hospital**
Supervised RN staff for 260-bed county hospital. Chaired shared governance and public health committees. Promoted after four years service as level III RN.

Education: MSN   Wake Forest University   1991
BSN   Western New England College   1989
AA   Newport Business College   1986

References: On request.

FUNCTIONAL RESUME

KEVIN SNYDER
439 Washington Street
Charleston, South Carolina 29425
Home: 803-555-4671
Office: 803-555-7721

Background

Ten years of nursing experience in hospital ICU and medical/surgical units. BSN plus critical care certifications.

Skills

- Primary patient care, including IV therapy, monitoring of vital signs, postoperative wound care, and pain management.
- Delegation to and supervision of nursing assistants, orientation of new staff, and monitoring of nursing students.
- Extensive voluntary participation in hospital's community-based health care programs, including blood drives, mobile immunization efforts, and public speaking engagements.

Employers

Charleston Medical Center
Level II Staff Nurse
2/98 to Present

St. Mary's Hospital
Per Diem Nurse
2/95 to 2/98

Education

BSN   South Carolina State College   1995
Certifications: TNS, CEN, ACLS

References available.

Remember that a resume is not an autobiography. Too much information will only get in the way. The more compact your resume, the easier it will be to review. If a person who is swamped with resumes looks at yours, catches the main points, and then calls you for an interview to fill in some of the details, your resume has already accomplished its task. A clear and concise resume makes for a happy reader and a good impression.

There are times when, despite extensive editing, the resume simply cannot fit on one page. In this case, the resume should be laid out on two pages in such a way that neither clarity nor appearance is compromised. Each page of a two-page resume should be marked clearly: the first should indicate "page 1 of 2," and the second should include your name and the page number, for example, "Julia Ramirez—page 2 of 2." The pages should then be stapled together. You may use a smaller font (in the same font as the body of your resume) for the page numbers. Place them at the bottom of page one and the top of page two. Again, spend the time now to experiment with the layout until you find one that looks good to you.

Always show your final layout to other people and ask them what they like or dislike about it, and what impresses them most when they read your resume. Make sure that their responses are the same as what you want to elicit from your prospective employer. If they aren't the same, you should continue to make changes until the necessary information is emphasized.

Proofreading

After you have finished typing the master copy of your resume and before you have it copied or printed, thoroughly check it for typing and spelling errors. Do not place all your trust in your computer's spellcheck function. Use an old editing trick and read the whole resume backward—start at the end and read it right to left and bottom to top. This can help you see the small errors or inconsistencies that are easy to overlook. Take time to do it right, because a single error on a document this important can cause the reader to judge your attention to detail in a harsh light.

Have several people look at the finished resume just in case you've missed an error. Don't try to take a shortcut; not having an unbiased set of eyes examine your resume now could mean embarrassment later. Even experienced editors can easily overlook their own errors. Be thorough and conscientious with your proofreading so your first impression is a perfect one.

We have included the following rules of capitalization and punctuation to assist you in the final stage of creating your resume. Remember that resumes often require use of a shorthand style of writing that may include sentences without periods and other stylistic choices that break the standard rules of grammar. Be consistent in each section, and throughout the whole resume, with your choices.

RULES OF CAPITALIZATION

- Capitalize proper nouns, such as names of schools, colleges, and universities; names of companies; and brand names of products.

- Capitalize major words in the names and titles of books, tests, and articles that appear in the body of your resume.

- Capitalize words in major section headings of your resume.

- Do not capitalize words just because they seem important.

- When in doubt, consult a manual of style such as *Words Into Type* (Prentice-Hall) or *The Chicago Manual of Style* (The University of Chicago Press). Your local library can help you locate these and other reference books. Many computer programs also have grammar help sections.

RULES OF PUNCTUATION

- Use commas to separate words in a series.

- Use a semicolon to separate series of words that already include commas within the series. (For an example, see the first rule of capitalization.)

- Use a semicolon to separate independent clauses that are not joined by a conjunction.

- Use a period to end a sentence.

- Use a colon to show that examples or details follow that will expand or amplify the preceding phrase.

- Avoid the use of dashes.

- Avoid the use of brackets.

- If you use any punctuation in an unusual way in your resume, be consistent in its use.

- Whenever you are uncertain, consult a style manual.

Putting Your Resume in Print

You will need to buy high-quality paper for your printer before you print your finished resume. Regular office paper is not good enough for resumes; the reviewer will probably think it looks flimsy and cheap. Go to an office supply store or copy shop and select a high-quality bond paper that will make a good first impression. Select colors like white, off-white, or possibly a light gray. In some industries, a pastel may be acceptable, but be sure the color and feel of the paper makes a subtle, positive statement about you. Nothing in the choice of paper should be loud or unprofessional.

If your computer printer does not reproduce your resume properly and produces smudged or stuttered type, either ask to borrow a friend's or take your disk (or a clean original) to a printer or copy shop for high-quality copying. If you anticipate needing a large number of copies, taking your resume to a copy shop or a printer is probably the best choice.

Hold a sheet of your unprinted bond paper up to the light. If it has a watermark, you will want to point this out to the person helping you with copies; the printing should be done so that the reader can read the print and see the watermark the right way up. Check each copy for smudges or streaks. This is the time to be a perfectionist—the results of your careful preparation will be well worth it.

Chapter 4

The Cover Letter

Once your resume has been assembled, laid out, and printed to your satisfaction, the next and final step before distribution is to write your cover letter. Though there may be instances where you deliver your resume in person, you will usually send it through the mail or on-line. Resumes sent through the mail always need an accompanying letter that briefly introduces you and your resume. The purpose of the cover letter is to get a potential employer to read your resume, just as the purpose of the resume is to get that same potential employer to call you for an interview.

Like your resume, your cover letter should be clean, neat, and direct. A cover letter usually includes the following information:

1. Your name and address (unless it already appears on your personal letterhead) and your phone number(s); see item 7.

2. The date.

3. The name and address of the person and company to whom you are sending your resume.

4. The salutation ("Dear Mr." or "Dear Ms." followed by the person's last name, or "To Whom It May Concern" if you are answering a blind ad).

5. An opening paragraph explaining why you are writing (for example, in response to an ad, as a follow-up to a previous meeting, at the suggestion of someone you both know) and indicating that you are interested in whatever job is being offered.

6. One or more paragraphs that tell why you want to work for the company and what qualifications and experiences you can bring to the position. This is a good place to mention some detail about

that particular company that makes you want to work for them; this shows that you have done some research before applying.

7. A final paragraph that closes the letter and invites the reviewer to contact you for an interview. This can be a good place to tell the potential employer which method would be best to use when contacting you. Be sure to give the correct phone number and a good time to reach you, if that is important. You may mention here that your references are available upon request.

8. The closing ("Sincerely" or "Yours truly") followed by your signature in a dark ink, with your name typed under it.

Your cover letter should include all of this information and be no longer than one page in length. The language used should be polite, businesslike, and to the point. Don't attempt to tell your life story in the cover letter; a long and cluttered letter will serve only to annoy the reader. Remember that you need to mention only a few of your accomplishments and skills in the cover letter. The rest of your information is available in your resume. If your cover letter is a success, your resume will be read and all pertinent information reviewed by your prospective employer.

Producing the Cover Letter

Cover letters should always be individualized, because they are always written to specific individuals and companies. Never use a form letter for your cover letter or copy it as you would a resume. Each cover letter should be unique, and as personal and lively as possible. (Of course, once you have written and rewritten your first cover letter until you are satisfied with it, you can certainly use similar wording in subsequent letters. You may want to save a template on your computer for future reference.) Keep a hard copy of each cover letter so you know exactly what you wrote in each one.

There are sample cover letters in Chapter 6. Use them as models or for ideas of how to assemble and lay out your own cover letters. Remember that every letter is unique and depends on the particular circumstances of the individual writing it and the job for which he or she is applying.

After you have written your cover letter, proofread it as thoroughly as you did your resume. Again, spelling or punctuation errors are a sure sign of carelessness, and you don't want that to be a part of your first impression on a prospective employer. This is no time to trust your spellcheck function. Even after going through a spelling and grammar check, your cover letter should be carefully proofread by at least one other person.

Print the cover letter on the same quality bond paper you used for your resume. Remember to sign it, using a good, dark ink pen. Handle the letter and resume carefully to avoid smudging or wrinkling, and mail them together in an appropriately sized envelope. Many stores sell matching envelopes to coordinate with your choice of bond paper.

Keep an accurate record of all resumes you send out and the results of each mailing. This record can be kept on your computer, in a calendar or notebook, or on file cards. Knowing when a resume is likely to have been received will keep you on track as you make follow-up phone calls.

About a week after mailing resumes and cover letters to potential employers, contact them by telephone. Confirm that your resume arrived and ask whether an interview might be possible. Be sure to record the name of the person you spoke to and any other information you gleaned from the conversation. It is wise to treat the person answering the phone with a great deal of respect; sometimes the assistant or receptionist has the ear of the person doing the hiring.

You should make a great impression with the strong, straightforward resume and personalized cover letter you have just created. We wish you every success in securing the career of your dreams!

Sample Resumes

This chapter contains dozens of sample resumes for people pursuing a wide variety of jobs and careers in the field of nursing, or who have had experience in this field in the past.

There are many different styles of resumes in terms of layout and presentation of information. These samples also represent people with varying amounts of education and work experience. Model your resume after these samples. Choose one resume or borrow elements from several different resumes to help you construct your own.

CHRISTINE WARD
1950 South Union Street
Melbourne, FL 32901
cward@xxx.com
407-555-8237

OBJECTIVE:
Charge or Triage Nursing Position in Trauma/ER Department

SKILLS:
- Document patient histories and status in various computer programs and databases
- Exercise sound judgment as triage nurse responsible for prioritizing cases and assigning staff
- Provide medical advice and poison control information by phone
- Initiate patient treatment and testing
- Schedule staff members and ensure adequate departmental staffing

EMPLOYERS:

Melbourne General Hospital	April 1999 to Present
Wharton Medical Center	May 1993 to April 1999
Lincoln Medical Center	June 1989 to May 1993

EDUCATION:
RN, St. Andrew's School of Nursing, 1987

References available

Scott Le Mans, MSN, CEN, TNS

59 North Macon Street
Harlingen, Texas 78550
Cellular Phone (210) 555-5968

Overview

Nurse manager with ICU, CCU, and home health experience. Coordinate scheduling and management of 15 employees for 20-bed ICU. Ensure department's compliance with JCAHO standards and all state and federal regulations. Monitor patients' treatment and status to ensure quality pre- and postoperative care. Maintain quality control standards through intensive orientation and ongoing program/service development.

Employers

6/97 - Present	Harlingen General Hospital, Nurse Manager Intensive Care Unit
5/92 - 6/97	Simpson Medical Center, Level II Staff RN Coronary Care Unit
6/90 - 5/92	Austin Home Health, Case Manager

Credentials

BSN Baylor University, 1990
Texas Nursing License 6817720-3
Trauma Nurse Specialist
Certified Emergency Nurse

References Available

Elizabeth Carr

4820 South Engwall Road
Forsyth, GA 31209
(912) 555-4225

Recent Experience

Educational Consultant, October 1999 to Present

Develop curriculum on contract basis. Recent clients include Forsyth Public Health Department and University of Georgia BSN Program.

Assistant Professor of Nursing, September 1996 to October 1999

Responsible for trauma nursing curriculum for University of Georgia's accredited BSN program, with a course load of four sections per semester. Received superior student and staff evaluations.

Director of Nursing, August 1994 to September 1996

Supervised nursing staff at St. Catherine's, a 500-bed facility. Carried out management and quality control responsibilities.

Education

MSN   Syracuse University, New York   1990

Certifications

Georgia Public Health Certificate
Georgia Nursing License 628-543164
American Heart Association Certification for Basic and Advanced Life Support
Member, Emergency Nurses Association
ENA Trauma Nursing Core Provider
Patient Database Maintenance Certification

References

Personal and professional references provided on request.

George A. Atkinson

411 Greenville Road
Eau Claire, Wisconsin 54702
GAAtkinson@xxx.com
715-555-9712

GOAL:
Medical Services Coordinator

SKILLS:
- Financial management and fund-raising experience
- Knowledge of JCAHO accreditation standards, state and federal guidelines
- Creation of procedural standards, quality control programs
- Knowledge of Medicare, Social Security, and Public Aid regulations
- Familiar with various computer programs to maintain patient files and insurance database

EMPLOYERS:
Stevenson Rehabilitation Clinic
Director
1/95 to Present

Northeast Community Hospital
Director of Nursing
1/92 to 1/95

CREDENTIALS:
MSN, University of Wisconsin, Whitewater, 1992
    Certifications: CPR, CEN, TNS, ACLS
    Member, American Nurses Association

REFERENCES:
Available on request

Christopher Wiley
862 Oak Street
Santa Clara, CA 95051
Home (408) 555-3948
Pager (408) 555-9881

Goal: Full-time pediatric nursing position

Background: Eight years of hospital nursing experience serving pediatric and geriatric patient populations. Direct patient care from assessment through discharge planning. Excellent peer reviews. Active committee member. Four years as home health case manager.

Employers:

Santa Clara Community Hospital Pediatric Staff Nurse	1/97 – Present
St. Andrew's Hospital for Children Pediatric Staff Nurse	2/94 – 1/97
Quality Home Health Inc. Case Manager	6/91 – 2/94

Credentials:
BSN, San Diego State, 1991
California Nursing License 843682
Pediatric Advanced Life Support Certification
CPR Certification
Member, American Nurses Association

Computer Skills:
Microsoft Excel, Word, and Outlook
Lotus Notes
Meeting Maker
Proficient in using Internet medical search engines

References: Available

THERESA FOSTER
916 South Wilkins Avenue
Reynoldsburg, Ohio 43068

Home: (617) 555-6879
Pager: (617) 555-6655

GOAL

Community mental health nursing

OVERVIEW

- Five years of community mental health nursing
- BSN, MSN in progress
- Extensive experience with pediatric and adolescent psychiatric cases
- Strong clinical assessment skills

EXPERIENCE

Glenview Hospital
Mental Health Nurse
September 1998 to Present

Northwest Community Mental Health Center
Outpatient Mental Health Counselor
July 1994 to September 1998

EDUCATION

Ohio Nursing License #583-126052
RN, St. Catherine's School of Nursing, 1994
BA, Psychology, Ohio State, 1990

REFERENCES

Personal and professional references on request

JANICE HARTSON

220 Prospect Street
McLean, VA 22102
(703) 555-7815
Pediatric Nurse Practitioner

WORK HISTORY

1998 – Present
Briar Street Clinic
Level II Staff Nurse. Provided routine outpatient care, community referral, and counseling at medical clinic averaging 20,000 visits annually.

1995 – 1998
McLean General Hospital
Level II Pediatric Staff Nurse. Acquired extensive experience with pediatric oncology cases. Acquired experience with plasmapheresis, IV therapy, pain control, symptom management, and grief counseling.

1990 – 1995
Gannon Medical Center
Level II RN, Neonatal ICU. Provided clinical nursing assessment and appropriate interventions for critically ill infants.

EDUCATION

MSN   University of Vermont 1990

CERTIFICATIONS/LICENSE

Certified by National Certification Board of Pediatric Nurse Practitioners
Pediatric Advanced Life Support Certified
CPR Certified
RN License 862-503126

AFFILIATIONS

Virginia Nurses Association
Society of Pediatric Nurses

REFERENCES

Collin White, Director
Briar Street Clinic
(703) 555-7382
cwhite@xxx.com

Susan Munroe, Director of Nursing
McLean General Hospital
(703) 555-6128, ext. 518

Scott Williams

1062 West Lemont Road • St. Louis, MO 63146 • 314-555-2269

OVERVIEW

Nurse advocate and labor relations specialist. Act as a collective bargaining representative and health care lobbyist. Personally and professionally committed to furthering the best interests of registered nurses and licensed practical nurses.

RECENT EXPERIENCE

1996 - Present
Director
Missouri Nurses Association
Primary focus is drafting and lobbying for legislation to protect collective bargaining rights of nurses and LPNs.

1993 - 1996
Labor Relations Specialist
Midwest Nurses Alliance
Represented alliance members in grievance procedures and contract negotiations. Investigated grievances. Educated chairpersons to assist them in representing their bargaining units.

1989 - 1993
Director of Education
Breslin Memorial Hospital
Responsible for staff orientation and certification programs, in-service workshops, nursing preceptor programs, and community health initiatives.

PUBLICATIONS

- "Job Security in the Age of Downsizing," *The Nurse Advocate*, November 1994.
- "Collective Bargaining: The Newest Strategies," *Journal of Holistic Health*, July 1997.
- "The Politics of Public Policy," *American Nurse*, February 1999.

EDUCATION

| MSN | University of Texas Health Science Center | 1989 |
| BSN | St. Catherine's College | 1987 |

CERTIFICATIONS

National Labor Relations Board

ANCC Advanced Nursing Administration

REFERENCES

Available upon request.

Elena Perez
2744 Covington Road
San Antonio, TX 78284
(210) 555-3964
E-mail: elenap@xxx.com

Nursing Skills

Primary care experience in neonatal ICU, newborn nursery, pediatric oncology unit, and pediatric medical/surgical unit.

Employers

St. Theresa's Hospital
Staff Nurse
Neonatal ICU
9/97 to Present

San Antonio Children's Hospital
Pediatric Staff Nurse
8/92 to 9/97

Lake Augusta Children's Camp
Summer Camp RN
5/89 to 8/92

Credentials

BSN, Villanova University, 1989
Texas Nursing License #682-738914
PALS Certified
Member, Society of Pediatric Nurses

References

Personal and professional references on request.

CHARLES KENDRICK

4182 Victoria Street
Dublin, CA 94568
Home: 510-555-7796
Cell: 510-555-2120
E-mail: kendrick57@xxx.com

OBJECTIVE

Community mental health nursing in hospital or clinic setting

EXPERIENCE

1/98 to Present
Dublin General Hospital and Medical Center
Crisis Counselor, Outpatient Mental Health

Provide group and individual counseling services in outpatient clinic. Responsible for 24-hour emergency rotation, recruitment, and training of volunteers. On call for ER to assist with clinical assessment of psychiatric cases, referral, and/or facilitation of transfer to appropriate facility.

5/92 to 1/98
Mercy Hospice
Grief Counselor

Counseled terminally ill patients and families. Oriented new staff members. Participated in community outreach, public speaking engagements, and fundraising. Served as an advocate for rights of the terminally ill.

EDUCATION

California Nursing License #218-730614

MSW	Rosary College	1992
RN	College of St. Catherine	1989

REFERENCES AVAILABLE

Christine Gleason

1811 Foley Street #602 • Washington, DC 20024
(202) 555-4113 • E-mail: cbgleason@xxx.com

Overview

RN with background as program coordinator and educational director desires position as educational director for local hospital or medical research foundation.

Employers

1997 - Present
Education Director
American Nurses Association
Washington, DC

1995 - 1997
Director of Development
Lexington Home Health Care
Lexington, KY

1988 - 1995
Charge Nurse
Richmond General Hospital
Richmond, VA

Skills

Public and media relations
Curriculum development
Nursing recruitment, orientation, and management

Computers

- Microsoft Office 2000 (Word, Excel, Outlook)
- Lotus Notes
- PageMaker
- QuarkXpress
- Familiarity with Internet search engines and on-line medical databases

Education

M.Ed.	Georgetown University	1991
B.S.N.	University of Virginia	1988

HENRY JENSON
488 Sterling Road
Richmond, KY 40475
Home: (606) 555-2067
Cell: (606) 555-7292
E-mail: jensen_h_t@xxx.com

BACKGROUND
BSN with experience in both hospital and home health settings. Oncology and cardiac care background. Ten years of nursing experience.

EXPERIENCE
Richmond Community Medical Center
Level II Staff Nurse, Oncology Unit   6/96 to Present

Responsible for all direct patient care including setup of infusion pumps, IV therapy, chemotherapy, and pain management. Educate and counsel patients and families. Interact extensively with radiologists and respiratory therapists.

St. Francis Hospital
Level II Staff Nurse, Cardiac Care Unit   8/94 to 6/96

Responsible for direct care of cardiac patients. Proficient in IV therapy, use of ventilators, intra-aortic balloon pumps, Swan-Getz catheters, and 12-lead EKGs. Assisted in Cardiac Rehabilitation Unit as requested.

Regency Nursing Agency
Per Diem RN   8/92 to 8/94

Agency nurse responsible for long- and short-term private-duty assignments serving a wide array of patients.

EDUCATION
BSN   Eastern Kentucky University   1992

References Available

SUSAN WRIGHT

1411 Harrod Lane
Boulder, CO 80304
Home: 303-555-4958
Pager: 303-555-6789
E-mail: suewright@xxx.com

GOAL

Entry-level RN position

EXPERIENCE

1997 to Present
Volunteer Nurse Assistant
Mercy Hospice

Assist nursing staff in providing primary care to terminally ill patients. Monitor patients' status and vital signs and report to nursing supervisor. Provide grooming and bathing assistance and emotional support for patients.

1994 to 1997
Medical Records Clerk
Bishop Hospital

Recorded patient histories and insurance information. Maintained computerized patient database. Gained extensive knowledge of medical terminology.

EDUCATION

Bishop Hospital School of Nursing
RN expected June 2002

CREDENTIALS

CPR certified
Member, American Student Nurses Association

REFERENCES

Carol Robinson
Nursing Coordinator
Mercy Hospice
303-555-7643, ext. 911
E-mail: carolrobinson@xxx.com

Sharon Caruso
Director of Medical Records
Bishop Hospital
303-555-7643, ext. 486

LISA JOHNSON

913 Lincoln Street • Okeechobee, Florida 34972
(941) 555-3285 • E-mail: Lisa345@xxx.com

Background

RN/EMT with extensive background in trauma services. Seeking full-time ER nursing position.

Experience

6/99 to Present
Wesley Memorial Hospital
ER nurse responsible for all phases of primary nursing care for level I trauma center receiving 30,000 visits annually. Triage patients and initiate treatment. Carry out physician's testing requests. Serve as committee member for quality assurance and volunteer training programs. Assisted with conversion from paper documentation to computerized charting using HELP system documentation program.

5/95 to 6/99
Clark County Community Rescue Service
Emergency medical technician and team leader for mobile trauma unit. Stabilized patients in the field and transported to ER. Trained dispatchers.

Education

Florida Nursing License 012-936474
RN Wesley Hospital School of Nursing   1999
AS   Emergency Medical Technology,
    Punta Gorda Community College   1995

Certifications
Mobile Intensive Care Nurse (MICN)
Trauma Nurse Specialist (TNS)
Certified Emergency Nurse (CEN)
Certified CPR Instructor

Computer Skills
Extensive knowledge of HELP system documentation program
Proficiency with Microsoft Office 2000

Affiliations
Emergency Nurses Association
Alliance of Trauma Care Providers

References Available

AUDREY WOODARD

946 Gates Street
McLean, VA 22102
(703) 555-6238
E-mail: nurseaudrey@xxx.com

OVERVIEW

BSN with eight years of hospital nursing experience, seeking full-time staff RN position in medical/surgical unit. Prefer day shift and opportunity to grow into supervisory role.

EXPERIENCE

New England General Hospital
Level II Staff RN
1/98 to Present

Medical/surgical staff RN in 500-bed hospital. Rotate to other floors as needed. Active member of pharmacy and shared governance committees.

Greenville County Hospital
Level II Staff RN
5/94 to 1/98

Provided primary care for postoperative patients. Supervised nursing students on clinical rotation.

CREDENTIALS

BSN, University of Vermont, 1994
Member, American Nurses Association

REFERENCES

Available on request.

BETSY LINDQUIST

625 South Henderson Street
Falmouth, MA 02541
(508) 555-1068
Cell: (508) 555-7364
E-mail: lindquistb@xxx.com

OBJECTIVE:
Occupational Health Nursing Position

SKILLS:
- Administer preemployment physical exams
- Test physical work ability
- Evaluate workers' compensation claims
- Assess workplace safety
- Develop and administer employee fitness and wellness programs
- Administer health care benefits programs
- Microsoft Office 2000
- Lotus Notes

EMPLOYERS:
New England Nurses Association
Workplace Advocate   6/97 to Present

The Leland Corporation
Health Care Coordinator   8/95 to 6/97

CREDENTIALS:
BSN   Medical University of South Carolina, College of Nursing, 1997
Member, American Nurses Association

REFERENCES AVAILABLE

Eileen McAdams

418 North Third Street
St. Louis, MO 63146
314-555-3626
E-mail: mcadams35@xxx.com

Goal:

Labor and delivery staff RN position

Credentials:

BSN, Avila College, Kansas City, 1996
Missouri Nursing License #975-987436
CPR and PALS certification
Member, Missouri Nurses Association

Experience:

1996 to Present
Labor and Delivery Staff Nurse
Stevenson Women's Hospital

Evaluate and triage patients upon admission. Monitor patients' progress and assist them with pain management techniques. Assist physicians with delivery. Care for healthy newborns in nursery. Instruct patients in breast-feeding and infant care techniques. Arrange discharge planning.

References:

Available on request

Linda Abramo
616 Winston Court
San Diego, CA 92123
Home: 619-555-1985
Cell: 619-555-7685

Objective:
Full-time pediatric staff RN position in a hospital setting

Experience:
Northwest Community Hospital
Pediatric Department
Level II RN, 6/96 to Present

Provided primary nursing care for patients in 20-bed pediatric department.

Center for Child Protection
Catholic Children's Hospital
Level II RN, 7/93 to 6/96

Staff RN for 50-bed pediatric unit specializing in child abuse recovery.

Credentials:
RN, Mercy Hospital School of Nursing, June 1993
California Nursing License #934-805413
PALS and CPR certified
Member, California Nurses Association

References:
Available

Duncan Farrell, RN, MSN

216 Wentworth Road
Boston, MA 02116
617-555-1050
E-mail: dfarrell@xxx.com

Experience

- Well-trained MSN with specialization in pediatric nursing
- Five years of experience in neonatal ICU unit at level II trauma center
- Research and publications
- PALS certification

Employers

Christian Children's Medical Center, Boston, MA
Level II Pediatric Staff Nurse   1/98 to Present

St. Martin's Hospital, Boston, MA
Level II Pediatric Staff Nurse   2/96 to 1/98

Liberty Hospital, Denver, CO
Level II Pediatric Staff Nurse   6/92 to 2/96

Credentials

Active RN licenses in Colorado (914-523256) and Massachusetts
  (907-441873)
BSN, Amherst University, 1992
RN, Newberry School of Nursing, 1989
Pediatric Advanced Life Support Certification

Research/Publications

Pediatric Hyponatremic Seizures: New Medication Strategies, research paper presented to American Association of Pediatric Nurses, Spring 1999 Convention.

"Pediatric Resuscitation Carts in the Neonatal ICU," *Emergency Nursing Bulletin*, January 1997, pp. 29–31.

References Available Upon Request

JADE WONG

494 Brook Street
West Lafayette, Indiana 47907
317-555-8460
E-mail: jade_wong@xxx.com

Pediatric Nurse Practitioner

Experience

Southwest Community Mental Health Service
Psychiatric Nurse Practitioner
2/97 to Present

Provide outpatient therapy at community mental health center. Responsible for 24-hour emergency service rotation; provide education and consultation to health care professionals and family caretakers.

Preston Adolescent Treatment Center
Level II Staff RN
6/94 to 2/97

Member of multidisciplinary treatment team serving adolescent women dealing with mental health issues, including substance abuse and eating disorders. Duties included patient observation and assessment, nursing diagnosis, care planning, counseling, and crisis intervention.

Hoffman House
Staff RN, 8/89 to 6/94

Staff RN for adult respite care center. Varied patient population included seniors with memory loss and limited mobility. Ensured safe, therapeutic environment for clients. Provided education and emotional support for primary caregivers.

Page 1 of 2

Education

BSN   Purdue University   1989
Major: Public Health

Affiliations

American Nurses Association
Midwest Alliance of Nurse Practitioners

References Available

Susan Ramos, MSN

986 Yates Street
Chicago, IL 60618
(312) 555-6978
Pager: (312) 555-3999
E-mail: ramos_sue@xxx.com

Work History

1/98 to Present, *Director of Education and Community Relations*
Bradley Medical Center

- Develop and implement all staff training, in-service programming, recertification programs.
- Supervise publication of in-house newsletter, press releases, and patient education literature.
- Design and direct marketing/community relations campaigns and special events.
- Serve as media contact/hospital spokesperson.

10/94 to 1/98, *Director*
Ridgeway Rehabilitation Center

- Directed daily operation of 50-bed residential substance abuse treatment center.
- Managed nursing and support staff.
- Assisted board of directors with long- and short-range budgets and planning.
- Directed fund-raising and community relations efforts.

8/92 to 10/94, *Assistant Professor*
St. Andrews College, BSN Program

- Taught public health nursing, pediatric nursing, and chemical dependency courses.
- Functioned as research assistant.
- Assumed responsibility for ongoing curriculum development.

6/90 to 8/92, *Level II RN*
Children's Hospital

• Served as pediatric staff RN for 250-bed hospital.
• Garnered a wide range of experience, including trauma, burn, and
  oncology cases.

Computer Proficiency

MS Word, Excel, Outlook
Netscape Navigator
Internet Explorer

Education

MSN	University of Illinois	1990
BSN	University of Delaware	1988

Credentials

Member, Illinois Nurses Association
Member, American Nurses Association
Illinois RN License #802-546931
Certified CPR instructor

References

On request

Mark D. Bradley

5895 Glendale Road
Lake Forest, CA 92630
(714) 555-4956

Work Experience

Nursing
- Level III staff RN for level II trauma/emergency department
- ICU/CCU experience on part-time, on-call basis
- Home health experience
- Quality assurance specialist

Teaching
- Instructor, Mobile Intensive Care Nurse course
- Curriculum consultant for Lake Forest Department of Public Health's paramedic training program

Supervision
- Charge nurse for level II trauma center
- Relief house supervisor for level II trauma center

Employers

Holy Cross Hospital	Level III Staff RN	1/97 to Present
Barrington Home Health	Agency RN	8/94 to 1/97
Alexis Medical Center	Charge RN	8/90 to 8/94

Education

| BSN | University of California, San Diego | 1990 |
| AS | Lakeland College | 1988 |

Certifications

California Public Health Certificate	
California Nursing License	RN495860
Basic and Advanced Life Support	American Heart Association
Certified Emergency Nurse	Emergency Nurses Association
Trauma Nursing Core Provider	Emergency Nurses Association
Member	California State Nurses Association

References Available

KAREN T. CHAPMAN

5612 East Central Street
Ann Arbor, MI 48106
(313) 555-7614
ktchapman@xxx.com

GOAL

Nursing Management

SKILLS

- Extensive background as Charge Nurse responsible for managing nursing staff to ensure prompt, high-quality nursing care.

- ER Triage Nurse with experience in assessing and prioritizing cases to facilitate smooth flow of patients and optimal use of nursing staff.

- Staff nurse positions in cardiac/telemetry and pediatric units.

- Active member of shared governance council.

- Arrange in-service presentations for nursing staff on varied topics, including self-defense for caregivers, HIV/AIDS updates, and child abuse detection.

- Knowledgeable in numerous computer programs for documenting patient history and stats; also proficient in Microsoft Word, Excel, and Access.

EMPLOYERS

Marist General Hospital
ER Charge Nurse and Triage Nurse
July 1997 to Present

St. Mary's Hospital
Staff Nurse:

- Cardiac/Telemetry Unit
  May 1994 to July 1997

- Pediatric Unit
  June 1990 to May 1994

CREDENTIALS

BSN, Michigan State University, awarded June 1990

TNS, ACLS, PALS, and CPR certified

REFERENCES

Personal and professional references are available.

ALICE K. WILLIAMSON

566 Courtney Lane
Uniondale, PA 18711
Cellular: 717-555-5958

OBJECTIVE

Home health position using my prior experience with oncology and cardiac patients

WORK HISTORY

Uniondale General Hospital 1/97 to Present

Level II Staff Nurse with experience in cardiac, oncology, and pediatric units. Responsible for direct patient care, charting, care plans, and discharge planning.

Camenson Home Health 2/93 to 1/97

Case Manager. Coordinated and monitored patient care and progress. Scheduled nursing care, ordered equipment, arranged social services consults and support services as needed. Maintained and reviewed charts to ensure compliance with all federal and state health care regulations.

CREDENTIALS

Pennsylvania Nursing License RN384850
Advanced Cardiac Life Support Certification
American Red Cross CPR Certification
Member, American Society of Nurse Managers

EDUCATION

BSN University of Washington–Seattle, 1/93

REFERENCES

Available on request

LYNN BENNETT

977 Calvert Road
Baltimore, MD 21202
Bennett634@xxx.com
Pager: (410) 555-1785

NURSING EXPERIENCE

9/96 to Present
ST. CATHERINE'S HOSPITAL AND MEDICAL CENTER
Neonatal Nurse Practitioner

Provide primary care to newborns—well and ill—in neonatal ICU and newborn nursery.

8/92 to 9/96
GARRETT CHILDREN'S HOSPITAL
Pediatric Staff Nurse

Provided primary care for pediatric patients in 200-bed children's hospital. Acquired extensive oncology and medical/surgical experience.

5/89 to 8/92
MORGAN MEDICAL GROUP
Pediatric Nurse

Provided primary care for private pediatric practice.

EDUCATION

BSN,   University of Baltimore   1989

AFFILIATIONS

Society of Pediatric Nurses
Maryland Nurses Association

REFERENCES

On request

SHANDELL WILLIAMS

682 Paxton Street • Grand Rapids, MI 49505
Cellular: 312-555-9684 • swilliams@xxx.com

Background

Professional RN with hospital nursing and home health experience. Seeking challenging staff nurse position with potential to grow into supervisory duties.

Skills

- Experienced oncology nurse familiar with plasmapheresis, pain control and symptom management, and counseling for terminally ill patients and their families
- Case management experience acquired as home health and private-duty nurse working to coordinate with community resources and services to ensure comprehensive patient care plans
- IV therapist
- ICU nurse capable of assessing and responding to cardiac emergencies

Work History

1998 - Present	St. Mary's Home Health	Case Manager
1995 - 1998	Spectrum Community Hospital ICU & Oncology Units	Level II RN
1991 - 1995	Jessup Personnel	Private-Duty Nurse

Education

RN	Kalamazoo School of Nursing	1991

Certifications
CPR
Advanced Cardiac Life Support

License
Michigan #283-394857

Affiliations
Michigan Nurses Association
National Council for Home Health Professionals

Computers
Proficient in Microsoft Office 2000, including Word, Excel, Meeting Maker, and PowerPoint. Also knowledgeable in numerous database programs used in area hospitals for tracking patient stats and history.

References
On request

Kimberly Levine

1620 Coleman Road • Butte, MT 40112 • Pager: (203) 555-2256

GOAL
Nursing Management Position

EXPERIENCE
First Street Women's Clinic
Nursing Supervisor, 1/98 to Present

Supervise nursing staff for women's clinic providing obstetric services and referral for more than 500 patients per year. Hire, train, and supervise nursing staff. Establish procedural standards. Monitor patient care and review documentation to ensure adherence to state regulations.

St. Michael's Care Home
Director of Nursing, 1/92 to 1/98

Supervised nursing staff for 500-bed long-term care facility. Responsible for staffing, training, and evaluation of nursing staff. Reviewed patients' medical status to develop and update individualized treatment programs. Established quality control program. Reviewed charting and care plans to ensure compliance with all Medicare, Social Security, and Public Aid requirements.

CREDENTIALS
BSN   Pine Brook College, 1992
Certifications: CPR, ACLS, TNS, PALS
Montana License # 478-384759
Member, Montana Nurses Association
Member, American Nurses Association

REFERENCES
Robin Woods
Director
First Street Women's Clinic
Work: (203) 555-6712
Cellular: (203) 555-7829

Warren McNeal
Chief Administrator
St. Michael's Care Home
Work: (203) 555-9003
E-mail: mcneal_stmichael@xxx.com

Laura R. Davis

462 Reckert Road
East Hampton, NY 11937
lauradavis@xxx.com
(516) 555-7382

• Goal

RN position in hospital or clinic setting.

• Experience

Fairview Medical Clinic
Staff RN
6/97 to Present

Provide varied health care services at community clinic serving 20,000+ patients annually. Services include blood pressure screening, pregnancy and AIDS testing, routine prenatal services, TB screening, and psychiatric services and referrals.

School District 32
School Nurse
8/93 to 6/97

District nurse on call for three elementary schools. Maintained student health records on district mainframe. Organized district-wide wellness and parent education programs.

• Credentials

BSN, East Hampton School of Nursing, 1993
AS, Biology, New England Community College, 1991
Member, American Nurses Association

References Available

Lucy Wang

2411 Keystone Road
Madison, Wisconsin 53716
lucywang@xxx.com
Cellular: (608) 555-3445

Skills

- Assess and triage patients
- Educate patients on pain management techniques
  during labor, postpartum care, breast-feeding, and newborn care
- Assist physicians with deliveries
- Perform primary nursing duties in newborn nursery
- Create comprehensive discharge plans

Credentials

BSN   University of Wisconsin, 1990
Wisconsin Nursing License #86410
CPR and PALS certifications
Member, Wisconsin Nurses Association

Employers

Madison Hospital
Labor and Delivery Nurse
June 1993 - Present

Women's Health Cooperative
Staff Nurse
July 1990 - June 1993

References

Personal and professional references on request

INDIRA PAX
988 Gavin Road
Newport News, VA 23606
Home (904) 555-8214
Cellular (904) 555-9602

Goal:
Management position in home health industry that will use supervisory and marketing skills.

Experience:

9/98 to Present
Director of Recruitment, NurseTemps Inc.
Direct marketing/recruitment program. Design direct mail campaigns. Produce promotional literature. Developed employee screening process currently in use. Monitor employee performance. Have increased staffing by 15 percent during past year.

8/95 to 9/98
Educational Director, St. Anne's Hospital
Responsible for staff orientation, peer review, and community outreach programs.

7/91 to 8/95
Director of Nursing, Morgan County Hospital
Supervised RN staff for 260-bed county hospital. Chaired shared governance and public health committees. Promoted after four years service as level III RN.

Education:

MSN	Wake Forest University	1991
BSN	Western New England College	1989
AA	Newport Business College	1986

References:
On request.

Pamela James, MSN

296 Birkland Court • Conifer, CO 11535 • (843) 555-7163 • pjames@xxx.com

Experience

9/97 to Present
Project Manager
Comprehensive Immunization Initiative
Colorado Nursing Foundation

Working to develop educational programs for health care professionals, design public health programs, and establish goals for improved immunization service and delivery to all children by age 24 months.

2/95 to 9/97
Educational Specialist
Helen White Nursing Scholar Program
National Nursing Academy

Assisted endowment director in reviewing scholarly abstracts to select recipients of grants in public health nursing.

1/92 to 2/95
Board Member
Colorado Board of Nursing

Appointed to serve state nursing board consulting on professional issues, including nursing licensure, disciplinary measures, school accreditation, and establishment of nursing practices and procedures.

Education

MSN   University of Denver   1992

REFERENCES AVAILABLE

STEVE SAUNDERS

6204 Nessett Circle
Denver, CO 80262
(303) 555-7338 Home
(303) 555-1993 Office
E-mail: saunders@xxx.com

OVERVIEW

Experienced occupational health nurse with prior CCU experience. BSN and critical care certifications along with eight years of nursing experience.

EXPERIENCE

Merrill Corporation
Occupational Health Nurse
2/98 to Present

Managed health care programs for corporation with more than 500 employees. Duties included preemployment exams, documentation of workers' compensation cases, establishment of corporate safety standards, and creation and implementation of employee wellness programs.

Denver General Hospital
Staff Nurse, Critical Care Unit
2/92 to 2/98

Responsible for general nursing duties for critically ill surgical, coronary, and posttrauma patients.

EDUCATION

BSN   University of Colorado School of Nursing, 1992
ACLS Certified
TNS Certified

REFERENCES ON REQUEST

Alex J. Kent
483 West Fairfield Road
Santa Clara, CA 95051
Home: 408-555-1382
Pager: 408-555-5270

GOAL: Nursing position with focus on serving posttrauma patient population. Interested in relocating to New York City or immediate vicinity.

EXPERIENCE: 4/92 to Present
Santa Clara Rehabilitation Institute
Staff Nurse II. Duties: General nursing responsibilities as member of multidisciplinary therapeutic team. Participate in development of treatment and discharge plans. Assess, monitor, and chart patient status. Assist physicians in performing diagnostic tests and providing treatment. Provide counseling, support, and education to patients and families.

9/91 to 3/92
Santa Clara YMCA
CPR Instructor. Duties: Trained community members in CPR techniques.

EDUCATION: BSN   St. Mary's College, March 1991
                 CPR and ACLS certification courses passed

LICENSE: California Nursing License #897-485757

AFFILIATIONS: California Nurses Association
                  American Nurses Association

REFERENCES AVAILABLE

Lisa K. Evans

1596 Piedmont Road • Durham, NH 03824
(603) 555-4206 • Pager: (630) 555-8237

GOAL:

Geriatric Nursing Position

OVERVIEW:

• Talented RN with experience on orthopedic surgery ward
• Compassionate pre- and postoperative care
• Proven ability to develop successful discharge plans, including strategies for coping with altered mobility
• Experience in hospital and skilled care settings
• Nursing preceptor

WORK RECORD:

11/98 to Present
Level II Staff RN
Durham Community Hospital

10/92 to 11/98
Staff RN
Leighton Skilled Care Center

CREDENTIALS:

New Hampshire Nursing License #108-57410
RN, Durham School of Nursing, 1992
Member, American Nurses Association

References Available

SUSAN E. WILDER

962 Redmond Road
Melbourne, FL 32902
407-555-0179
swilder@xxx.com

BACKGROUND

Nurse educator seeking tenure track assistant or associate professor position at nationally recognized research university.

RECENT EXPERIENCE

Florida State University
Center for Nursing Practice
Assistant Professor of Nursing
1996 - Present

Responsible for maternal-child courses for RN-BSN program.

Melbourne Memorial Hospital
Education Specialist
1993 - 1996

Implemented nursing orientation and preceptor programs. Developed and oversaw community health education programs.

St. Francis Care Center
Director of Nursing
1989 - 1993

Managed nursing staff for 50-bed substance abuse recovery program.

RESEARCH

Currently completing ongoing prevention and behavioral research at Florida State University regarding HIV-positive newborns.

Recently awarded ANA grant to pursue research on clinical issues and trends in early intervention for developmentally delayed infants.

PUBLICATIONS

"Beating the Odds: Prenatal Care and Teenage Mothers," *American Nurse*, October 1994.

"Discharge Planning for the Addicted Newborn: Assuring Quality Care in the Home," *Social Services Weekly*, June 1995.

EDUCATION

MSN	University of Missouri	1984
BSN	Marycrest College	1980

CERTIFICATIONS

PALS
CPR
ACLS
TNS

REFERENCES AVAILABLE

ALICE SANSONE   6576 Elizabeth Court   Home: (508) 555-8325
                    Falmouth, MA 02541   Office: (508) 555-9415

BACKGROUND

- Experienced hospital administrator
- Strong employee relations and arbitration skills
- Proven record of cost containment and quality control
- Successful facilities management

WORK HISTORY

1997 - Present
Administrative Director
Falmouth General Hospital, Falmouth, MA

Assist chief administrator in directing all activities of this 300-bed facility. Duties include personnel management, fiscal management, and public relations.

Achievements

- Initiated fund-raising effort that increased hospital endowment by $1.5 million

- Designed new community outreach projects to enhance hospital's visibility and image in the community

1991 - 1997
Assistant Hospital Administrator
Perkins Memorial Hospital, Richmond, VA

Responsible for fiscal management, human resources, and facilities management projects under supervision of chief administrator.

Achievements

- Instituted new data processing procedures that increased collections and facilitated third-party reimbursements.

- Directed construction of $25 million maternal/child care wing that increased admissions by 20 percent. Responsible for all aspects of project: funding, contract negotiations, project management. Project completed on time and within budget.

EDUCATION

MBA   Harvard University   1991
BSN   University of Virginia 1989

References Available

CLARENCE T. JACKSON

3316 Westview Road
Lake Forest, CA 92630
tjackson@xxx.com
(714) 555-6150

OVERVIEW

Experienced EMT capable of responding to wide variety of trauma cases at scene. Currently seeking RN licensure. Strong commitment to career in trauma services.

EDUCATION

BSN   Nursing
University of California, degree expected 2002

AS   Emergency Medical Technology
Lake Forest Community College, 1993

Board-Certified EMT

CPR Instructor

EXPERIENCE

Lake Forest Community Rescue Team   *1995 to Present*

Team leader for urban mobile trauma unit. Interface with hospital ER staff by phone to provide trauma management en route from accident scenes. Stabilize patients for transport. Train dispatchers to answer calls and document critical information.

Warren County Fire and Rescue Service   *1993 to 1995*

CPR instructor for firefighters and EMTs. Provided CPR certification programs for community groups as requested.

REFERENCES AVAILABLE

MARCIA BLAKE

5082 Merrick Street • Union, KY 41091 • Cellular: (606) 555-6315

Background

- BSN with more than 10 years of nursing experience
- Staff RN for pediatric and med/surg units
- Mental health counselor for psychiatric hospital
- MSN in progress

Employers

UNION HOSPITAL
Staff RN
1994 - Present

Perform primary nursing duties for 30-bed pediatric unit. Rotate to med/surg unit as needed.

BRENTWOOD PSYCHIATRIC INSTITUTE
Mental Health Nurse
1990 - 1994

General nursing, patient assessment, and counseling duties for psychiatric hospital specializing in pediatric and adolescent psych cases.

Education

Kentucky Nursing License #484-123026
MSN   in progress Union College, degree expected 2002
BSN   St. Catherine's College, 1990

Computer Skills

Familiar with current computer programs used in regional medical facilities for documenting patient insurance information, recording stats, and logging medical history. Extensive work with patient database maintenance at Union Hospital. Also proficient in Microsoft Office 2000, including Word, Excel, Access, and PowerPoint.

REFERENCES AVAILABLE

Kevin Park

4316 Lincoln Street
Dallas, Texas 75243
(214) 555-9406
kpark@xxx.com

Goal:

Opportunity to combine counseling skills and nursing education in position as crisis worker/RN in hospital or clinic setting

Skills:

- Volunteer recruitment and training
- Thorough knowledge of crisis intervention techniques
- Grief counseling experience
- Public relations skills
- Fund-raising and grant-writing abilities
- Public speaking experience

Employers:

Administrative Director
Kerrington Hospice
January 1998 to Present

Direct all activities for local hospice serving over 2,000 clients per year. Responsible for establishing annual budget, recruiting and training staff, organizing community relations activities, fund-raising, scheduling, counseling, and serving as liaison to local hospitals.

Director of Public Relations
Dallas General Hospital
May 1991 to January 1998

Responsible for producing hospital newsletter, representing hospital at community events, organizing community health programs, issuing press releases, and reporting to the press.

Education:

RN in progress, degree expected June 2002
Dallas General Hospital School of Nursing

BA in Communications, January 1991
Southern Methodist University

Computers:

PageMaker
QuarkXpress
Photoshop

Affiliations:

National Society of Mental Health Practitioners
Student Nurses of America

References:

On request

Feliciana Valenzuela
BSN, MSN, CEN

9659 Dreyer Street • Santa Fe, NM 80204
E-mail: valenzuela@xxx.com • Pager: (303) 555-4507

Education

MSN   University of New Mexico, 1996
BSN   University of New Mexico, 1993

TNS, CEN, ACLS certified
Member, Emergency Nurses Association

Work History

4/96 to Present
Nurse Manager/Emergency Department
Kaiser Medical Center, Santa Fe, NM

Responsible for 24-hour management of emergency department services. Accountable for 25-bed ED with annual census of 40,000+ patients. Coordinate activities and fiscal management of 50 employees. Ensure departmental compliance with hospital and JCAHO standards and regulations. Report directly to the assistant administrator.

3/93 to 4/96
Clinical Nurse Specialist
Jameson General Hospital, Santa Fe, NM

Worked in 40-bed ED/trauma center receiving 60,000 visits per year. Performed patient education, administered program/service development on hospital computer programs, and initiated quality improvement programs.

2/91 to 3/93
Trauma Nurse
Wexler Memorial Hospital, Santa Fe, NM

Triage and charge nurse for level I trauma center.

References

Personal and professional references available.

Ellen K. Scott

283 Stapen Street
Atlanta, Georgia 30301
(404) 555-4494
ellenscott@xxx.com

SUMMARY
- BSN with six years of full-time hospital nursing experience
- MSN in progress
- Seeking challenging nursing position with opportunity to acquire supervisory skills

EMPLOYMENT HISTORY
St. Catherine's Hospital, Atlanta, Georgia
Level II RN
January 1994 to Present

Level II RN in 600-bed facility. Primary duties on pediatric floor, but float to medical and surgical unit as needed to fill staffing shortages. Administer medications and assist staff physicians with treatment. Perform patient education and discharge planning responsibilities. Active member of volunteer training and quality control committees. Currently work part-time while completing MSN.

Northeastern Community Hospital, Richmond, Virginia
Level II RN
May 1990 to January 1994

Level II RN in postoperative unit. Implemented various postoperative care plans. Supervised LPNs. Taught patient education classes. Performed discharge planning.

EDUCATION
MSN   Georgia State University, degree expected June 2002
BSN   University of Virginia, March 1990

REFERENCES AVAILABLE

Carolyn Meggett, RN

2140 Howe Street • Weston, MA 02193 • Cellular: (831) 555-4653

Goal
Emergency Nursing

Experience
4/96 to Present
ER Charge Nurse
Valley View Hospital

- Coordinate all patient care activities. Work with ER attending physicians to organize systematic flow of patients, expedite delays, and provide optimal care for patients and efficient use of nursing staff.
- Maintain communication and positive rapport with patients, families, and other hospital departments.
- Handle MICU telemetry calls, poison control calls, and medical advice calls.
- Maintain adequate staffing, handle sick calls, and coordinate resource response team coverage for cardiac and multiple trauma patients.
- Maintain adequate inventory of supplies; order or secure additional supplies as needed.

3/92 to 4/96
ER Triage Nurse
Wyeth Hospital

- Assisted charge nurse in maintaining flow of patients and providing appropriate, timely care.
- Communicated patient status and admission or discharge plans to patient and/or family.
- Obtained patient histories and documented patient status and physicians.
- Initiated treatment, providing first aid, ordering X-rays, etc.
- Maintained communication with charge nurse, support staff, patients, and families.
- Notified police on reportable cases.
- Restocked triage supplies.
- Assisted with telemetry calls as needed.

Page 1 of 2

Credentials
RN   Wyeth School of Nursing 1992
TNS (Trauma Nurse Specialist)
CEN (Certified Emergency Nurse)
State of MA Nursing License #615-147782

References
Personal and professional references available and forwarded on request.

Nancy Zimmerman

1275 Hadfield Road
Jackson, MS 80216
Pager: (803) 555-8300
Home: (803) 555-2771

Background

- More than 10 years of experience in public health nursing
- Committed to patient advocacy and social reform
- Experienced, effective mental health counselor

Employment

1995 - Present
Mental Health Counselor
Center Clinic, Jackson, MS

Counsel adolescent and adult women in one-on-one and group settings. Provide a safe and therapeutic environment for women confronting depression, low self-esteem, domestic violence, substance abuse, and other mental health issues. Chart patient progress daily and weekly. Develop long- and short-term therapeutic goals. Provide referral to other agencies and services as necessary. Serve on clinic board of directors.

1991 - 1995
Assistant Director
New Hope Women's Shelter, Ottawa, MS

Assisted director with all aspects of clinic management from fund-raising and long-term planning to daily operation of clinic. Recruited and trained volunteers, managed 24-hour telephone hotline, and assisted with counseling of residents. Admitted new residents and assessed their physical and mental state. Helped design and staff on-site child care program.

Page 1 of 2

1988 - 1991
Public Health Nurse
Ottawa County, Ottawa, MS

Treated patients on-site and at two clinic locations. Assisted patients with home health needs: arranging for equipment, home health aids, or application for residential care. Diverse patient population and wide range of patient needs provided experience in everything from early childhood immunizations to hospice care.

Education

Augustana School of Nursing   RN   1988

University of Washington   BA   1986
Double major in Psychology and Sociology

Credentials

Mississippi RN license 856-121341
Red Cross CPR certification
Member, American Nurses Association

References Available

Bruce Zampieri

3160 MacGregor Drive
Jefferson City, Missouri 55180
(521) 555-1701
brucezampieri@xxx.com

Goal

A challenging pediatric nursing position with room for advancement.

Background

- More than 10 years of experience in pediatric nursing, including neonatal intensive care responsibilities.
- Strong commitment to professional development, including design and presentation of in-service workshops, active involvement in Pediatric Nurses Association, and ongoing research on pediatric emergency issues.
- Prompt, accurate patient assessments and holistic approach to patient care.

Employment History

Lexington Children's Hospital
St. Louis, Missouri
Level II Pediatric Nurse
1998 to Present

Provide direct patient care in busy 10-bed neonatal ICU at Level One trauma center. Triage, assess, and treat patients. Conduct routine neurological assessments. Monitor and chart patients' progress, dispense medication, and provide IV therapy.

Page 1 of 2

**St. Mary's Medical Center
St. Louis, Missouri
Level II Pediatric Nurse
1994 to 1998**

Pediatric oncology nurse on 12-bed unit. Participated in chemotherapy treatments. Educated and supported patients' families. Interacted extensively with radiology and respiratory therapy staff.

**Union Hospital
Carson City, Missouri
Level II Pediatric Nurse
1989 to 1994**

Acquired wide range of pediatric experience on 15-bed unit.

Education

University of Missouri
BSN in Nursing, 1989

Certifications

CPR and TNS certified
Licensed in the state of Missouri (686-357297)

References

Personal and professional references are available upon request.

TIM BRYANT

2130 Marquis Drive • St. Louis, MO 63146
Office: (314) 555-1183 • Cellular: (816) 555-6277

CREDENTIALS

State of Missouri nursing license #687-358290
RN, Triton School of Nursing, 1993
Member, National Association of Orthopedic Nurses
CPR and ACLS Certified

WORK RECORD

Bennington Community Hospital
Orthopedic Staff Nurse
10/97 to Present

Care for geriatric patients on orthopedic surgery ward. Prepare patients for surgery and provide postoperative care. Assist patients with discharge planning and developing long-term strategies for dealing with altered mobility.

Trenton Nursing Center
Staff Nurse
8/93 to 10/97

Provided skilled nursing care at 250-bed long-term care facility; experienced with geriatric Alzheimer's patients. Trained LPNs. Presented staff workshops on various topics, including "sundowning" syndrome in Alzheimer's patients and self-defense techniques for caregivers.

REFERENCES

Katie Edelberg
Director of Nursing
Bennington Community Hospital
(314) 555-2922
E-mail: edelberg_kate@xxx.com

Barbara Higgins
Director of Human Resources
Trenton Nursing Center
(314) 555-6857

KEVIN SNYDER
439 Washington Street
Charleston, South Carolina 29425
Home: 803-555-4671
Office: 803-555-7721

Background

Ten years of nursing experience in hospital ICU and medical/surgical units. BSN plus critical care certifications.

Skills

- Primary patient care, including IV therapy, monitoring of vital signs, postoperative wound care, and pain management.
- Delegation to and supervision of nursing assistants; orientation of new staff; and monitoring of nursing students.
- Extensive voluntary participation in hospital's community-based health care programs, including blood drives, mobile immunization efforts, and public speaking engagements.

Employers

Charleston Medical Center
Level II Staff Nurse
2/98 to Present

St. Mary's Hospital
Per Diem Nurse
2/95 to 2/98

Education

BSN   South Carolina State College   1995
Certifications: TNS, CEN, ACLS

References available.

CECILIA RUIZ

1921 Willowbrook Road   (314) 555-1170
Columbia, MO 65212   cruiz@xxx.com

Goal

Emergency nursing management

Highlights

- BSN from University of Virginia, 1985
- Licensed in Virginia (#118-142037) and Missouri (#868-347124)
- Five years of clinical experience
- CPR and ACLS certified
- Nursing instructor

Employment

1992 - Present	Trauma Nursing Instructor Columbia School of Nursing Columbia, MO
1991 - Present	Trauma Services Coordinator Mosby Hospital Columbia, MO
1986 - 1991	Nurse Practitioner St. John's Medical Center Richmond, VA
1985 - 1986	Level III Trauma Nurse Children's Hospital Washington, DC

Achievements

- Manage 10 RNs, LPNs, and support staff at 200-bed regional medical center
- Served as delegate to Emergency Nurses Association Conference, 1995 and 1996
- Presented paper, *Pediatric Cardiovascular Emergencies*, at ENA Scientific Assembly, 1996
- Received Award for Professionalism from Mosby Hospital Board of Directors, 1996

References

Provided on request

WILLIAM ACUNA

202 Bedford Lane
Roselle, Illinois 60172
(708) 555-8162 Home
(708) 555-3571 Cellular

Background: Professional health care manager who provides sound business leadership while creating an environment conducive to compassionate patient care.

Skills:

Business
- Sales
- Budgetary Control
- Marketing
- Purchasing

Supervisory
- Employee Recruitment
- Performance Evaluations
- Training
- Scheduling

Employers:

1996 - Present
Director, Harrison Home Health
Elmhurst, Illinois

Direct all aspects of agency. Develop and implement marketing plan. Ensure compliance with all state and federal regulations. Purchase all durable medical equipment. Develop and monitor annual budget.

1991 - 1996
Personnel Director, St. Catherine's Skilled Care Center
Mount Prospect, Illinois

Responsible for all aspects of human resources for staff of 20+ health care workers. Duties included hiring, training, supervising, scheduling, and evaluating employees.

Page 1 of 2

1989 - 1991
Level III RN, Rosary Hospital
Park Ridge, Illinois

Provided direct patient care in pediatrics and medical/surgical departments.

Education: BSN, University of Illinois, Chicago, 1989
Minor in Accounting

Affiliations: Illinois Nurses Association
Society of Health Care Managers

References: Available on request

Stephanie Bowman

1910 Hardy Street
Honolulu, Hawaii 96814
Home: 808-555-6668
E-mail: sbowman@xxx.com

GOAL

Nursing program management responsibilities in either a clinic or a hospital setting using my skills in mental and public health nursing.

WORK HISTORY

Keahou Clinic, Honolulu, Hawaii
Substance Abuse Counselor
1997 - Present
Provide one-on-one and group counseling to adolescent clients in private substance abuse treatment program. Recruit and train volunteers for crisis hotline. Develop and present educational programs at local high schools to encourage students to remain drug-free.

Edgewater Hospital, Sacramento, California
Managing Director, Outpatient Mental Health Clinic
1992 - 1997
Staff RN, 1990 - 1992
Directed outpatient mental health program serving approximately 80 clients per year. Program provides outpatient counseling, monitors patients' drug and psychotherapy regimes, and assists with placement in supervised living situations. Duties included staffing, scheduling, and giving reports to attending psychiatrists. Promoted after serving two years as staff RN in program, taking histories and assisting with office management.

Clayton Associates, Sacramento, California
Staff RN
1988 - 1990
Staff RN for physicians group in general practice. Assisted with direct patient treatment: charted status, took histories, provided treatment; assisted with patient scheduling as needed; provided home care instructions.

Arrowhead School, Monterey, California
School Nurse
1986 - 1988
Provided on-site routine and acute care as needed and assisted with ongoing health programs. Maintained students' health care files; provided health bulletins for parents and guardians.

EDUCATION

Licensed in the state of California (427-583215) and Hawaii (661-326335)

RN	Monterey School of Nursing	1986
BS	Kenyon College, Psychology	1983

REFERENCES

Personal and professional references provided on request.

Ellen Janssen

724 Olympia Drive • Des Moines, IA 50265
Home: (319) 555-1284 • Pager: (319) 555-6744

Overview

Licensed Iowa RN with experience in private practice and community health. Excellent interpersonal, communication, and marketing skills. Strong rapport with patients. Holistic approach to health care.

Work Experience

Planned Parenthood, Des Moines, IA
Reproductive Counselor
1993 - Present

Provide reproductive counseling at walk-in clinic serving 500+ clients per year. Provide one-on-one patient education regarding birth control and pregnancy. Assist with general office management, including patient scheduling and maintenance of computer database and files. Participate in short- and long-term planning of program. Monitor changes in federal health care law and implement procedural changes as necessary.

LifeSource, Des Moines, IA
Blood Drive Coordinator
1990 - 1993

Contacted corporations to request off-site blood drives. Set up equipment and supervised blood drives at corporate sites. Took donor histories, supervised LPNs and RNs, provided discharge instructions to donors. Assisted with in-house donations as necessary, including patient intake, scheduling, and telemarketing efforts to increase donations.

Capital Medical Group, Iowa City, IA
Staff Nurse
1987 - 1990

General duty nurse for pediatric practice. Provided standard well-baby care, such as immunizations and oral polio treatments, as directed by physicians. Took patient histories, assessed and charted conditions, completed necessary paperwork, and maintained patient files.

Education

BSN   Public Health University of Iowa 1987

References

Rachel Stern, Director
Planned Parenthood
(319) 555-6102
E-mail: stern_pp@xxx.com

Dr. Michael Cooper
Capital Medical Group
(319) 555-6123
E-mail: michaelcoopermd@xxx.com

James K. Melton

784 Crest Avenue • San Antonio, TX 78284 • Jamesmelton@xxx.com • (723) 555-1889

Goal

Management of daily operation and long-range planning for midsize medical clinic or nonprofit health care corporation.

Abilities

- Financial Planning
- Cost Containment
- Staffing
- Marketing
- Systems Analysis
- Grant Writing

Work Experience

General Manager, 1997 - Present
Ridgeway Medical Clinic

Director, 1993 - 1997
Garner Medical Center

Assistant Administrator, 1990 - 1993
Dallas Community Mental Health Program

Education

MBA   University of Texas, 1989
RN   Larrabee School of Nursing, 1985
Member, Texas Nurses Association
Member, National Academy of Health Management
Red Cross CPR Certification
Texas Nursing License #214-476182

Computer Experience

Proficient in Microsoft Office 2000, including Access, PowerPoint, Excel, and Word. Familiar with PageMaker, Adobe Photoshop, and QuarkXpress. Also familiar with a variety of database management systems and other office management software.

References Available

EDITH SLAVINSKI, RN

8976 Sierra Road
Newport News, Virginia 23606
Home: (804) 555-5958
Pager: (804) 555-7775

SKILLS

- Specialized trauma nursing
- General medical/surgical nursing
- Orientation of new staff
- Creation and presentation of in-house continuing education and certification programs
- Community referral
- Knowledge of computer database programs currently being implemented in local hospitals

CREDENTIALS

BSN from University of Virginia, 1988; graduated with honors; financed 80 percent of tuition by working full-time while carrying full course load

Certifications: CPR, ACLS, TNS, CEN, MICN

Virginia State Nursing License #325-595848

Memberships: American Nurses Association, Emergency Nurses Association

EMPLOYERS

St. Catherine's Hospital	Level III ER Nurse	1996 - Present
Drexler Memorial Hospital	Level II ER Nurse	1993 - 1996
Drexler Memorial Hospital	Level II Medical/Surgical Nurse	1990 - 1993

References Available

ANGELINA BROWNE

418 BRADLEY STREET
BAY CITY, MI 48706
517-555-5967
angiebrowne@xxx.com

OVERVIEW

*Licensed RN and labor relations specialist with diverse experience in health educa-
tion. Interested in challenging in-house position with nursing association or union.*

WORK HISTORY

1996 - Present
Labor Relations Specialist

Self-employed labor relations specialist. Participate in contract negotiations as the
collective bargaining representative for RNs. Successfully negotiated four labor
agreements during the past year, all including an increase in hourly wages.

1992 - 1996
President
Michigan Nurses Association

Directed professional nursing organization with 5,500 members and an annual budget of $250,000. Recruited members, supervised publication of monthly newslet-
ter, directed daily operation of office, and coordinated continuing education efforts
and special events.

1988 - 1992
Educational Director
Lutheran General Hospital

Managed all educational programs. Developed orientation materials and in-service
programming. Monitored staff certification and provided recertification programs
in-house and off-site. Supervised production of in-house newsletter and patient
education literature.

WORK HISTORY (CONT.)

1986 - 1988
Part-time Lecturer
Saginaw College BSN Program

Taught maternal and child care courses in accredited BSN program. Responsible for two sections and up to 40 students per semester. Received excellent student and peer reviews.

QUALIFICATIONS

MSN   Wayne State University   1986
BSN   Central Michigan University   1984
Michigan Nursing License   411-608542
National Labor Relations Board Certification
Member, American Nurses Association
Member and Past President, Michigan Nurses Association

REFERENCES

Susan Riley
President
Michigan Nurses Association
517-555-1629 Office
517-555-8990 Cellular

Karen LoBianco
Director of Nursing
Lutheran General Hospital
517-555-6100 Office

MARILYN SMITH
418 Whitesburg Street
Wauconda, IL 60084
708-555-9822

OBJECTIVE

Nurse Assistant Position

EMPLOYMENT

1994 - Present
Nurse Assistant
Pinkerton Nursing Center, Gary, IN

Report to RNs regarding patients' status and current needs. Assist patients with bathing and grooming needs. Monitor and record fluid intake and output, vital signs, general changes in mood or appearance. Promote patients' mental and physical health while assisting nursing staff.

1992 - 1994
Office Assistant
Kusler Medical Group, Merrillville, IN

Maintained database of patient files, answered phones, scheduled appointments, typed correspondence. Provided general clerical support for busy pediatric practice.

EDUCATION

Nursing Assistant Certification
Columbia Vocational Institute, 1992

COMPUTERS

Familiar with numerous word processing, presentation, and database programs, including Microsoft Office 2000 and Lotus Notes.

REFERENCES

Available on request

GREG STIMSON

1037 West Robin Road • Austin, TX 78768
(254) 555-8718 • gregstimson@xxx.com

EMPLOYMENT
1996–Present   St. Joseph's Hospital
                  Emergency Department RN Level III

- Responsible for all aspects of direct patient care at this level I trauma center with annual census of 32,000 patients
- Preceptor for new employees
- Public safety liaison
- Active member of education, public safety, and certification committees; coordinated in-service presentations on topics such as domestic violence, elder abuse, AIDS education, and self-defense for caregivers

1994–1996   Hennessey Hospital Medical Center
                 Emergency Department RN

- Direct patient care
- Extensive community referral
- Liaison to community mental health center affiliated with the hospital

Medical/Surgical RN

- Responsible for general pre- and postoperative care on 30-bed floor

CERTIFICATIONS/LICENSE
Advanced Cardiac Life Support (ACLS)
Certified Emergency Nurse (CEN)
Trauma Nurse Specialist (TNS)
Mobile Intensive Care Nurse (MICN)
Texas Nursing License #062-778019

EDUCATION
Hennessey Hospital School of Nursing, RN, 1994

AFFILIATIONS
Member, Emergency Nurses Association
Texas Nurses Association

References available on request

Pamela Grant, RN
411 Highland Court
Brookings, SD 57007
(605) 555-3889

Employment History

1998 - Present
Director, Corneal Transplant Program
South Dakota State University Eye Clinic

Manage corneal transplant program. Duties include tracing donors through nationwide computer database, supervising tissue typing, arranging the harvesting and transport of donor organs, counseling donor families, and obtaining formal consents. Direct clerical staff of two. Designed and implemented community outreach plan to increase awareness of need for donor organs.

1993 - 1998
Level III Trauma Nurse
St. Patrick's Hospital, Emergency Department

Provided full range of trauma nursing services in emergency department with annual census of 25,000 patients. Facilitated SDSU organ donations when possible, counseling families and securing initial consents. Developed in-service program to educate staff on obtaining organ donation consents.

1990 - 1993
Level II Staff Nurse
St. Patrick's Hospital, Neonatal Intensive Care

Provided direct patient care to critically ill newborns in six-bed neonatal intensive care unit. Assessed, monitored, and charted patient status. Implemented treatments and administered medications as directed. Provided patient education and emotional support for family members.

Education

BSN   South Dakota State University   1990

Certifications

TNS   Trauma Nurse Specialist Certification
CEN   Certified Emergency Nurse
ACLS   Advanced Cardiac Life Support

South Dakota State Nursing License #345-687958

References

Both personal and professional references are available upon request.

JOHN B. STEVENSON

2529 Endar Road • Cleveland, Ohio 44106
(216) 555-1197 Home • (216) 555-8091 Cellular

BACKGROUND

Talented nurse experienced in the areas of home health, oncology, acute coronary care, and hospice care seeks challenging full-time nursing position with successful home health agency.

WORK HISTORY

HTL Home Health Ltd.
Oncology Nurse
1994 - Present

Work in conjunction with physicians, social workers, therapists, and attendants to provide complete home care for oncology patients. Administer home treatments, including chemotherapy, IV antibiotic therapy, and IV pain management. Monitor and chart patients' progress. Develop ongoing care plans. Facilitate transitions to and from hospital care.

William and Mary Medical Center
Level II CCU Nurse
1991 - 1994

Provided primary care to cardiac patients in 15-bed coronary care unit. Identified cardiac rhythms. Monitored cardiac rehabilitation. Assisted with outpatient pulmonary/cardiac rehabilitation.

WORK HISTORY (CONTINUED)

Green Mountain Hospice
Intake Coordinator
1987 - 1991

Handled admissions for hospice program serving up to 20 clients per year. Cooperated with hospital and nursing home staff to arrange transition into hospice program. Explained hospice philosophy and services to clients and their families. Assisted families in seeking financial assistance and community services.

CREDENTIALS

BSN   Case Western Reserve   1987
ACLS and CPR Certified

PUBLICATIONS

"Dying at Home: Home Health Options for the Terminally Ill," *American Journal of Nursing*, July 1995

"Today's Hospice," *Hospice News*, May 1994

REFERENCES

Available on request

Kevin Ishida

622 Robinson Road   (708) 555-6123 Home
Des Plaines, IL 60016   (708) 555-8127 Work
                                                      kishida@xxx.com

Goal: *Teaching position with university or educational foundation.*

Expertise: Nursing experience in hospital and clinic settings. Member of multi-disciplinary rehabilitation team for patients with spinal cord injuries. Nursing supervisor for hospital and outpatient substance abuse programs.

                   Teaching and curriculum development experience at the university level.

                   Implementing new technology and training staff on effective archiving.

                   Clinical researcher conducting ongoing analysis of the effect of behavior modification techniques on substance abuse.

Credentials: MS in Nursing, University of Florida, 1990

                   BSN, Central Florida University, 1988

                   Member, American Nurses Association

Employers: 1993 - Present
                   Assistant Professor
                   Elmhurst College BSN Program

                   Teach psychosocial nursing, medical ethics, and research methods. Supervise nursing students in on-site clinical rotations. Conduct extensive research. Have input into department's ongoing curriculum development.

Page 1 of 2

1990 - 1993
Nursing Supervisor
Rehabilitation Institute of Daytona

Supervised staff of 30 RNs at rehabilitation facility providing comprehensive care for patients recovering from spinal cord injuries. Developed care plans in conjunction with psychology, occupational therapy, and physical therapy professionals. Responsible for staff scheduling, evaluations, in-service presentations, patient education, and discharge planning.

1988 - 1990
Head Nurse
Lambert Treatment Center

Nursing supervisor for outpatient substance abuse program monitoring patients in transition from inpatient to outpatient care. Supervised staff and developed treatment programs. Directed community education and outreach efforts.

References Available

Susan Lund

1225 Camden Road
Columbus, Ohio 43266
(614) 555-8316

Background

Dedicated, experienced RN seeking supervisory nursing position that uses my clinical, organizational, and human relations skills.

Previous Employment

November 1995 - Present
Covington General Hospital, Columbus, Ohio
Level IV Staff RN
Intensive Care Unit Supervisor

Charge nurse for 10-bed ICU. Supervise RNs, LPNs, and therapists. Facilitate implementation of multidisciplinary care plans. Schedule, train, and evaluate nursing staff. Carry out day-to-day directives of hospital administration.

April 1991 - November 1995
Good Shepherd Hospital, Milwaukee, Wisconsin
Level III Staff RN
Medical/Surgical Nurse

Observed, charted, and monitored patients' conditions. Assisted MDs with assessment and treatment. Provided general pre- and postoperative care. Developed discharge plans and instructed patients in home care.

May 1989 - April 1991
Lincoln Medical Center, Milwaukee, Wisconsin
Staff RN

Provided general nursing care at walk-in clinic, including community referral services, mental health and substance abuse interventions, and well-baby care. Instructed patients in home care and preventive health measures.

Page 1 of 2

Credentials

University of Wisconsin, BSN, 1989
Licensed in Wisconsin (394-362392) and Ohio (775-760381)
Member, American Nurses Association

References

A list of references will be provided on request.

MATTHEW CHANG
245 Bishop Street
Boulder, Colorado 80209
303-555-1936
mattchang@xxx.com

OBJECTIVE

Seeking entry into the dynamic field of home health care.

EXPERIENCE

Wesley Memorial Hospital,
512 Cutler Street, Denver, Colorado 80209

1993 - Present
Level III Staff RN for 10-bed Acute Coronary Care Unit
with 50 percent patient turnover daily

- Provide primary care to critically ill adult patients suffering from a wide range of cardiac diseases. Extensive experience with ventilators, intra-aortic balloon pumps, Swan-Getz catheters, and cardiac rhythm identification.

- Proficient in IV insertion, infusion of vasoactive drugs and phlebotomy, and 12-lead EKGs.

- Conduct in-services on pain assessment, radiological assessment of line placement, and physicians order entry system.

- Cross-trained to assist in six different units: surgical intensive care, endocrine/GI, pulmonary/renal, general surgical, monitored cardiac rehabilitation, and outpatient pulmonary/cardiac rehabilitation.

- Successfully implement cost containment procedures, resulting in a 90 percent reduction of lost revenue.

- Delegate responsibilities as needed in role of charge nurse.

EXPERIENCE (CONTINUED)

1990 - 1993
Level III RN for Acute Dialysis Plasmapheresis Unit.

• Delegate to the American Nephrology Nurses Association National Conference, 1992, in Washington, DC.

1989 - 1990
Level II RN for Endocrine/GI Unit.

EDUCATION

Received Diploma of Nursing from St. Francis Hospital School of Nursing in 1988. Earned 80 percent of educational expenses while working part-time and maintaining full course loads. Currently pursuing BSN through Colorado University.

CERTIFICATION

ACLS and CPR certified

OTHER

Currently work one shift a month in pulmonary cardiac rehabilitation.

References Are Available

Lee Ann Kusaka

3984 Briar Street
Oakland, California 94609
Home: (414) 555-2837
Cell: (414) 555-0098
E-mail: lakusaka@xxx.com

EDUCATION

M.S. in Public Health Administration, 1991
University of Hawaii

B.S. in Psychology, 1989
University of California, Berkeley

EXPERIENCE

General Manager
St. Mary's Medical Center
Oakland, California
1998 - Present

Direct day-to-day operations and long-range planning for medical clinic with annual budget of $2.5 million. Areas of responsibility include financial planning, cost containment, and staffing.

Achievements
- Increased first-year profits by 10 percent
- Continue to maintain steady financial growth
- Implemented marketing plan that resulted in a 15 percent increase in patient referrals from private physicians

Assistant Director
Lakehurst Recovery Center
San Francisco, California
1995 - 1997

Supervised medical records, admissions, and billing departments for substance abuse center with staff of 60.

EXPERIENCE (cont.)

Achievements (Lakehurst Recovery Center)
- Streamlined billing procedures
- Reduced annual operating expenses by 5 percent

Assistant Administrator
Northwest Mental Health Center
Berkeley, California
1992 - 1995

Assisted general manager of 60-bed psychiatric center. Participated in all aspects of health management: educational, therapeutic, and personnel. Involved in hiring and training of new staff members and volunteers. Assisted in direct patient care and emergency intervention as needed. Responsible for all billing.

Achievements
- Successfully recruited and trained group of 12 new volunteers
- Secured a $250,000 federal grant for research in obsessive compulsive disorders
- Implemented HELP computer program for the entire center

AFFILIATIONS

California Public Health Council
American Management Association
National Academy of Office Administrators

REFERENCES

Available on request

KAREN GREEN

486 Kramer Road • Uniondale, PA 18711
Work: (717) 555-9878 • Home: (717) 555-8102
Cell: (717) 555-9988

Experienced RN with demonstrated skill in quality control, utilization review, cost containment, program coordination, and collaboration with both medical staff and hospital administration.

PROFESSIONAL EXPERIENCE

Hewlett Rehabilitation Center, Uniondale, PA
Educational Director
1998 - Present

Responsible for all aspects of staff education for 320-bed hospital. Conduct utilization reviews. Develop guidelines for peer review and train supervisors in review strategies. Develop and implement training for new staff and in-service programs for existing staff. Create orientation manuals and supplementary educational materials. Monitor staff certification and licensure status, and schedule in-house certification programs in basic skills areas such as CPR.

Futura Home Health Inc., Cleveland, OH
Intake Supervisor
1996 - 1998

Reviewed patient applications to determine needs and insurance eligibility. Took patient histories, reviewed medical records, and collaborated with hospital and nursing home discharge planners. Scheduled equipment deliveries and nursing, therapy, and social work visits. Created and updated individualized care plans. Conducted patient review meetings with staff. Hired, trained, and evaluated RNs, LPNs, and therapists for program.

Taft General Hospital, Cleveland, OH
Staff/Charge Nurse
1993 - 1996

Staff RN and charge nurse for several departments, including medical/surgical, intensive care, and coronary care. Managed up to 35 patients and staff of up to five nurses and LPNs.

CERTIFICATIONS AND AFFILIATIONS

Registered Nurse, Pennsylvania and Ohio

Member, Pennsylvania Nurses Association
Director, Membership Committee
1998 - Present

Member, National Council of Health Care Professionals
Delegate to national convention
1993 - 1998

EDUCATION

BSN   Kent State University   1993

REFERENCES

Personal and professional references available.

Janice Biedermann

2190 Emerson Street
Concord, MA 01742
(508) 555-5133
E-mail: biedermann@xxx.com

AREAS OF NURSING EXPERTISE
- Oncology
- Hermatology
- Cardiac Care
- Home Health

SKILLS
- ACLS and CEN certified with experience in cardiac care units
- Experienced oncology nurse, comfortable in both home health and hospital settings
- Proficient in administration of chemotherapy and IV therapy, including home setup of infusion pumps
- Skilled hematology nurse: draw blood; dispense whole blood, platelets, and cryoprecipitate; insert and maintain venous catheters

EMPLOYMENT
Home Health
Oakdale Home Health Care
1997 - Present
Home Health Oncology Nurse

Hospital
Liberty General Hospital
1992 - 1997
Staff Nurse
Hematology and Oncology

Health Temps
1990 - 1992
Agency Nurse

EDUCATION
University of Massachusetts BSN 1990

REFERENCES AVAILABLE

Sally Wells

453 Pratt Lane
Atlanta, Georgia 30301
(404) 555-3130
Pager: (404) 555-5674
sallywells@xxx.com

Objective:

Psychiatric nursing position, with eventual supervisory potential, in a hospital or clinic setting.

Work History:

1998 - Present   **Level II RN**
Atlanta General Hospital **Psychiatric Services**

Provide all routine patient care. Assist with patient assessments. Dispense medication. Assist with group therapy. Attend staff meetings. Develop general care and discharge plans.

1994 - 1998   **Staff Nurse**
Covington House   **Substance Abuse Program**

Assisted patients with emotional and physical problems related to substance abuse. Designed and implemented individualized rehabilitation programs. Served as admissions liaison to local hospitals.

1991 - 1994   **Counselor**
Wheatley Mental Health Center **Adolescent Mental Health**

Provided group and individual counseling to adolescents in crisis. Designed and presented in-service programs for high school counselors.

Education:

University of Georgia   BSN   1991
Major: Nursing
Minor: Psychology
Licensed to practice nursing in the state of Georgia
  (#862-123026)

Affiliations:

Georgia Nurses Association
Southern Nurses Council

References:

On request.

Chapter 6

Sample Cover Letters

This chapter contains many sample cover letters for people pursuing a wide variety of jobs and careers in the field of law, or who have had experience in this field in the past.

There are many different styles of cover letters in terms of layout, level of formality, and presentation of information. These samples also represent people with varying amounts of education and work experience. Model your cover letter after these samples. Choose one cover letter or borrow elements from several different cover letters to help you construct your own.

Ms. Elizabeth Rodriguez
President
Professional Nurses of New England
418 Valley View Road
Rockville, MD 20849

June 24, 20--

Dear Ms. Rodriguez:

I was excited to learn of your current search for a successor because I believe I am uniquely qualified to continue your fine record of service to the nursing community in New England. As the enclosed resume indicates, I have an MSN, NLRB certification, and previous experience as a labor relations specialist and president of my state nursing organization. I'm sure you will agree that this diverse job experience would enable me to succeed in a number of key areas, including:

• Contract Negotiations
• Membership Recruitment
• Direction of Educational Efforts
• Supervision of Publishing Projects

I understand that your search for applicants will continue through the end of the month. I hope to hear from you after you have completed the arduous task of screening candidates. Should you wish to interview me at that point, I would be pleased to travel to Rockville at your convenience.

I appreciate your serious consideration of my qualifications and wish you good luck in your search for a new president.

Sincerely,

Angelina Browne
418 Bradley Street
Bay City, MI 48706
517-555-9301
angiebrown@xxx.com

EDITH SLAVINSKI, RN

8976 Sierra Road
Newport News, Virginia 23606
Home: (804) 555-5958
Pager: (804) 555-7775

TO: Mr. Philip Weston
           Director of Nursing
           New Haven General Hospital
           876 Brookside Drive
           New Haven, Connecticut 06510

DATE: May 17, 20--

RE: Application for Emergency Nursing Position

Our conversation this morning regarding the new emergency department at New Haven General was most enjoyable and informative. It is heartening to know that in this era of downsizing some health care institutions are still managing to thrive. With the extra space, equipment, and staff, the hospital can look forward to doing an even better job of serving the New Haven community.

I am excited at the prospect of becoming part of that process and glad to hear that there may be room for me on New Haven's ER staff. Here is my resume, which explains in more detail the things we touched on over the phone. If any other questions should arise before our meeting on May 29, give me a call at (804) 555-5958. I will be at home during the next few weeks, helping my family prepare for the move to Connecticut.

Two of my former supervisors have agreed to provide references for me. They are Judith Shaw at St. Catherine's, (804) 555-6978, and Warren Peterson at Drexler Memorial, (804) 555-3958.

I appreciate your taking the time to review my credentials and look forward to meeting you on the 29th.

Sincerely,

Edith Slavinski

Mr. Patrick Cross
Human Resources Director
Alzheimer's Task Force
411 Kearney Road
McLean, VA 22101

July 15, 20--

Dear Mr. Cross:

It is rare to find a professional opportunity that allows one to dedicate time to a cause that has great personal meaning. For me, serving as the educational director for the Alzheimer's Task Force would be both professionally and personally rewarding. My background in health care education qualifies me for the job, and dealing with Alzheimer's in my own family has given me a special understanding of the challenges caregivers face.

The enclosed resume provides the details of my work history. I am fortunate to have had a wide variety of experience as a health care educator. As a result, my communications skills are strong. My writing, public relations, and media relations abilities would serve me well in developing the media campaign and educational materials you require.

Please let me know if you need further information in order to consider me for this opening.

I would enjoy meeting you in person to discuss how we might join forces to battle Alzheimer's disease.

Sincerely,

Christine Gleason
1811 Foley Street #602
Washington, DC 20024
(202) 555-4113
E-mail: cbgleason@xxx.com

TO: Emily Richardson, Director
Whitfield Women's Clinic
411 Robinson Street
Park Ridge, IL 60648

FROM: Ellen Janssen
724 Olympia Drive
Des Moines, IA 50265

DATE: May 17, 20--

RE: Application for Charge Nurse Position

I enjoyed meeting you at the Women's Health Fair at Columbia College last weekend, and I am most interested in the charge nurse position you mentioned.

Here is the resume you requested, which details my nursing and educational background. Community health nursing is familiar territory for me, as you can see. Working in women's health care has also been a priority, which is why I've been working for Planned Parenthood.

I think my skills are a good match for the charge nurse position and hope that you agree. You can reach me at home at (319) 555-1284 or on my pager at (319) 555-6744 to arrange an interview. I'm enthusiastic about the possibility of working for you at Whitfield Women's Clinic and appreciate your interest.

Best wishes,

Ellen Janssen

Stephanie Bowman

1910 Hardy Street
Honolulu, Hawaii 96814
Home: 808-555-6668
E-mail: sbowman@xxx.com

March 16, 20--

Lucy Tanaka, Director
Children's Health Foundation
2719 Hamilton Street
Honolulu, HI 96814

Dear Ms. Tanaka:

I have tremendous admiration for the work your organization is doing in bringing health care to underprivileged children. Nothing would please me more than contributing to that effort by joining your staff as the assistant director. I feel well qualified for the position, having extensive nursing and health care program management experience.

Please review the enclosed resume and let me know if you need any other information to consider me for the assistant director position. I would also appreciate an interview if you feel my credentials warrant serious consideration. You may reach me at home on Tuesday and Thursday (555-6668) or at work on Monday, Wednesday, and Friday (555-9112).

I feel confident that I would make an excellent addition to your staff and look forward to the opportunity of working with you at the Children's Health Foundation.

Sincerely,

Stephanie Bowman

Sally Wells

453 Pratt Lane
Atlanta, Georgia 30301
(404) 555-3130
Pager: (404) 555-5674
sallywells@xxx.com

June 16, 20--

Ms. Susan Parker
Director of Nursing
McKeon Memorial Hospital
912 Central Street
Charlotte, North Carolina 28210

Dear Ms. Parker:

I enjoyed our conversation at last week's meeting of the Southern Nurses Council, and I would appreciate the opportunity to talk to you further about nursing positions at McKeon Memorial.

As you know, I currently work at Atlanta General as a level II psychiatric nurse. I have also worked in a residential substance abuse treatment center and an outpatient community mental health center. The enclosed resume sketches out my work history and extensive computer skills.

Your research into adolescent substance abuse treatment intrigues me and is just one reason that I'm interested in working with you. Please let me know if there is any way I can contribute to the health care team at McKeon.

Cordially,

Sally Wells

WILLIAM ACUNA

202 Bedford Lane
Roselle, Illinois 60172
(708) 555-8162 Home
(708) 555-3571 Cellular

May 28, 20--

Mr. Mark Kiely, Director
Munroe Nursing Center
Hanover Park, Illinois 60103

Dear Mr. Kiely,

The position you recently advertised in the *Chicago Tribune* seems to match my skills exactly. I am currently responsible for the management of a midsize home health agency—Harrison Home Health. The managerial skills I have developed at Harrison would translate well to the general manager position you're seeking to fill.

The enclosed resume explains my professional accomplishments in more detail. My salary requirements are negotiable.

I will contact you early next week to arrange an interview. Meanwhile, thank you for your consideration.

Sincerely,

William Acuna

SUSAN WRIGHT

1411 Harrod Lane
Boulder, CO 80304
Home: 303-555-4958
Pager: 303-555-6789
E-mail: suewright@xxx.com

May 6, 20--

Dr. Kevin Donovan, Director
Mercy Hospice
654 Winston Court
Boulder, CO 80304

Dear Dr. Donovan:

I am writing to request that you formally consider me for the entry-level RN position that just became available at Mercy Hospice.

As you know, I have worked at Mercy for the past five years as a volunteer nurse assistant. I would like to continue my efforts at Mercy as a full-time staff member after graduating from nursing school next month.

I have enclosed my resume for your review. Carol Robinson, who has been my direct supervisor, knows of my interest in the current nursing opening and is willing to discuss my credentials with you.

Thank you for your consideration. I hope that I can continue my successful association with Mercy this summer as your new staff RN.

Sincerely,

Susan Wright

James K. Melton
784 Crest Avenue • San Antonio, TX 78284 • Jamesmelton@xxx.com • (723) 555-1889

April 24, 20--

Ms. Regina Newcomb
Director of Human Resources
University of Texas Medical Center
2200 Augusta Drive
San Antonio, TX 78284

Dear Ms. Newcomb:

Managing health care institutions has never been a greater challenge. As more federal budget cuts loom, only careful financial stewardship will allow medical centers to provide quality care at reasonable cost. As the new director of your outpatient mental health clinic, I will provide the leadership necessary to make the coming years profitable for both the university and the community it serves.

The enclosed resume provides the details of my professional background, and I would appreciate the opportunity to discuss my qualifications in person. I will call early next week to arrange an interview.

Thank you for reviewing my credentials. I look forward to establishing a mutually beneficial association.

Sincerely,

James K. Melton

Mark McKenna
Managing Editor
Nursing News
1800 Glenwood Road
Boston, MA 02116

June 20, 20--

Dear Mr. McKenna:

As an avid reader of your magazine, I was pleased to learn of your search for a new assistant editor. My professional background includes a unique mix of editorial and nursing experience that makes me especially well qualified for the position.

I've enclosed a copy of my resume so that you may review my credentials. I also am available at your convenience for an interview. It is easiest to reach me in the mornings at work. The number there is 617-555-1202. You may also reach me by cell phone at 617-555-5546.

Beyond the skills described on my resume, I bring a high degree of dedication and dependability to my employers. I currently work part-time as the assistant educational director at Boston General. My supervisor there, Gloria Preston, is aware of my need for a full-time position and therefore supportive of my job search. You may contact her at 617-555-1204 for a reference.

Please let me know if you need any further information in order to consider me for the assistant editor position. I am sure that I would find it both personally and professionally rewarding to join the staff at *Nursing News*.

Yours truly,

Michael Schneider, RN
418 Long Street
Boston, MA 02116
617-555-5546
E-mail: mlshneider@xxx.com

Forum Home Health Care
348 Bennet Road
Cleveland, Ohio 44106
ATTN: Rosemary Best, Human Resources Specialist

April 16, 20--

Dear Ms. Best:

Like so many other nurses, I've shifted from hospital nursing to home health. For me, home health provides the best means to offer patients professional, compassionate, holistic care. I know that Forum Home Health Care shares these values. Several nursing colleagues, including Amanda Preston and Elizabeth Walsh, have shared with me their positive work experiences with your agency.

I am writing to introduce myself on the chance that you may have room for me on your staff. I am an experienced nurse whose background includes home health oncology nursing and hospice care. The enclosed resume provides amplification, and both Ms. Preston and Ms. Walsh are familiar with my work should you need a reference.

Thank you for taking time to consider my credentials. I look forward to the possibility of working with you at Forum.

Sincerely,

John B. Stevenson, RN
2529 Endar Road
Cleveland, Ohio 44106
(216) 555-1197 Home
(216) 555-8091 Cellular

Mr. Paul Ashecroft, Director
Jackson Park School of Nursing
1349 Greenville Road
Chicago, IL 60690

November 3, 20--

Dear Mr. Ashecroft:

As I was reading this month's issue of *The American Nurse*, I spotted your advertisement for nursing faculty. I am enclosing my resume and a list of references so that you may consider me for the psychosocial nursing position.

I have been a nurse educator for nearly a decade, as outlined in my resume. My experience encompasses instruction, clinical nursing practice and supervision, and research. Various aspects of my professional background uniquely qualify me for this position:

• Extensive clinical experience through my positions at Lambert Treatment Center and Rehabilitation Institute of Daytona

• Strong research skills, as evidenced by my receipt of a research grant from the American Nurses Foundation

• Effective teaching skills developed through instruction of students, staff, and patients in university, hospital, and clinic settings

• Proficient computer skills that include Microsoft Office 2000 and Lotus Notes

I am confident that my skills would enhance the faculty of Jackson Park, and I look forward to speaking with you in person.

Thank you for your consideration.

Sincerely,

Kevin Ishida
622 Robinson Road
Des Plaines, IL 60016
(708) 555-6123 Home
(708) 555-8127 Work
E-mail: kishida@xxx.com

Sylvia K. Warren
121 Waverly Place
Boston, MA 02129

May 15, 20--

Mr. Robert Pellum
Nursing Supervisor
Kingston Memorial Hospital
2602 Barrington Road
Boston, MA 02129

Dear Mr. Pellum:

I submit the enclosed resume in response to your advertised appeal
for a level II general surgical RN. Please note that my nursing background exactly matches your current needs. With more than five
years of successful service in hospital surgical nursing, I would
bring a wealth of experience to Kingston Memorial.

My long-term career goal is to gain supervisory experience, and I
have already demonstrated leadership ability by organizing numerous in-service programs for my current employer, Boston General.
Robin White, my current supervisor, has indicated her willingness
to act as a reference. Please feel free to contact her at 555-8311,
extension 216.

It is easiest to reach me at home at 555-2716, after 3 p.m.

Thank you for your consideration. I look forward to hearing from
you.

Yours truly,

Sylvia K. Warren

Mr. John P. Bowen
Alexandria Home Health Care
1619 Farragut Avenue
Chicago, IL 60645

October 5, 20--

Dear Mr. Bowen:

I have a consistent record of providing quality care to my patients.
My supervisors tell me they value the skill and dedication I bring to
my job as a nurse assistant. Patients appreciate my concern for their
emotional and physical needs.

Is your organization currently in need of nursing support? If so, I
would appreciate hearing from you. I am available during the day at
708-555-9822, and I have enclosed a resume for your review.

Please let me know of any openings at Alexandria for which I might
qualify.

Thank you,

Marilyn Smith
418 Whitesburg Street
Wauconda, IL 60084

Pamela Grant, RN
411 Highland Court
Brookings, SD 57007
(605) 555-3889

May 24, 20--

Ms. Ann Nguyen, Director of Personnel
Harrison Medical Center
7245 S. Campbell Street
Madison, WI 53792

Dear Ms. Nguyen:

As nursing becomes increasingly challenging and high-tech, health care providers are demanding the most qualified personnel possible. Harrison Medical Center is no exception, as your recent ad for a clinical transplant coordinator indicates. I feel confident that I could meet the high standards you set for your nursing staff, and I would enjoy the challenge of managing the daily operation of your transplant program.

My qualifications for the position are explained in detail in the enclosed resume. The highlights are as follows:

- Successfully manage corneal transplant program at the SDSU Eye Clinic. Number of donors has increased by 20 percent during my tenure.
- Additional transplant work as certified Trauma Nurse Specialist with more than four years of experience in hospital emergency room.
- BSN degree from South Dakota State University.
- Extensive database management, which assists in tracking donors and reduces paperwork.

I am willing to relocate and am eligible for RN licensure in the state of Wisconsin.

Please let me know if you need further information to evaluate my credentials. I look forward to discussing how I might contribute to the future success of Harrison's Clinical Transplant Program.

Cordially,

Pamela Grant, RN

Lee Ann Kusaka
3984 Briar Street
Oakland, California 94609
Home: (414) 555-2837
Cell: (414) 555-0098
E-mail: lakusaka@xxx.com

April 17, 20--

Ms. Lucy Eisenberg, Director
Hathaway House
418 Pearson Street
Oakland, California 94609

Dear Ms. Eisenberg:

Please consider me for the general manager position advertised in the *Oakland Gazette*. The enclosed resume provides the details of my experience as a health care coordinator.

Your advertisement called for an experienced clinic director with strong financial planning and patient management skills, as well as extensive computer skills. I meet these requirements and am interested in devoting myself to the day-to-day management of Hathaway House.

May I present my qualifications in person? You may reach me at (414) 555-2837 or on my cell phone at (414) 555-0098 to arrange an interview.

Cordially,

Lee Ann Kusaka

Ms. Melissa Wright
Herrington Home Health Care
1411 Grant Street
Denver, Colorado 80209

June 16, 20--

Dear Ms. Wright:

It was with great interest that I learned of your need for an intake counselor. I have been watching for such an opening at a home health agency, and I would like to apply for the position.

I have extensive nursing experience, as outlined in the enclosed resume. My background encompasses a wide cross section of medical specialties and a number of skills that would transfer well to the position of intake counselor:

• Recording patient histories
• Providing referral services
• Developing discharge plans
• Implementing cost containment procedures
• Proficiency in MS Office software, as well as Lotus Notes and Meeting Maker

I am confident that my abilities match your current requirements. May I call next week to arrange an interview so that we can discuss how I could contribute to your health care team?

Sincerely,

Matthew Chang
245 Bishop Street
Boulder, Colorado 80209
303-555-1936
mattchang@xxx.com

KAREN GREEN

486 Kramer Road • Uniondale, PA 18711
Work: (717) 555-9878 • Home: (717) 555-8102
Cell: (717) 555-9988

June 11, 20--

Mr. David Corolla
Director of Personnel
St. Vincent's Hospital
620 Riverview Drive
Gradyville, PA 19039

Dear Mr. Corolla:

A colleague of mine, Carlos Gestoso, suggested that I write to you regarding job opportunities at St. Vincent's. I work with Carlos at Hewlett Rehabilitation Center in Uniondale. As you probably know, Hewlett is closing its doors at the end of this calendar year, so I am seeking new professional opportunities.

Are you in need of an experienced RN with proven skills in educational development, quality control, and cost containment? If so, my resume should interest you. I have served as the educational director at Hewlett since 1998. My previous experience includes intake supervision and staff nursing in a variety of medical departments.

I will call early next week to see whether you would like to arrange an interview. You may reach me at work, (717) 555-9878, from 9 A.M. to 5 P.M. My home phone is (717) 555-8102, and you can also reach me via cell phone at (717) 555-9988.

Thanks for considering my credentials.

Sincerely,

Karen Green

GREG STIMSON

1037 West Robin Road • Austin, TX 78768
(254) 555-8718 • gregstimson@xxx.com

May 8, 20--

Ms. Melissa Trenton
Director of Nursing
Culverton General Hospital
1402 Larson Road
Culverton, VA 12245

Dear Ms. Trenton:

I enjoyed talking to you this morning regarding nursing opportunities at Culverton General and appreciate being able to interview with you during my visit on the 20th of this month. As a Virginia native, I know of Culverton's excellent reputation in the community and would be pleased to be associated with the hospital. Your current opening in the emergency department seems especially well suited to someone with my skills, as you can see from the enclosed resume.

I have been an ER nurse since 1994 and enjoy the challenge of working in emergency medicine. My current position at St. Joseph's Hospital has provided me with a wide range of trauma nursing experience. In addition to my on-the-job training, I have pursued extensive continuing education credits by attending in-service programs and attaining several specialized certifications such as TNS and CEN.

Of course, these details tell only part of the story. My strongest assets as a nurse are my rapport with patients and their families and my professionalism in working as a member of a team. I hope to put these qualities to work for you at Culverton General.

If any questions arise before the 20th, I am available before 3 P.M. at (254) 555-8718. I look forward to meeting you.

Sincerely,

Greg Stimson, RN